The 5 "As": Acceptance, Affection, Appreciation, Approval, and Attention

The 5 "As":
Acceptance, Affection, Appreciation, Approval, and Attention

✦

The Journey to Emotional Fulfillment.

Dyan Yacovelli, Psy.D.

iUniverse, Inc.
New York Lincoln Shanghai

The 5 "As": Acceptance, Affection, Appreciation, Approval, and Attention
The Journey to Emotional Fulfillment.

Copyright © 2008 by Dyan Yacovelli

All rights reserved. No part of this book may be used or reproduced by any means, graphic, electronic, or mechanical, including photocopying, recording, taping or by any information storage retrieval system without the written permission of the publisher except in the case of brief quotations embodied in critical articles and reviews.

iUniverse books may be ordered through booksellers or by contacting:

iUniverse
2021 Pine Lake Road, Suite 100
Lincoln, NE 68512
www.iuniverse.com
1-800-Authors (1-800-288-4677)

Because of the dynamic nature of the Internet, any Web addresses or links contained in this book may have changed since publication and may no longer be valid.

The information, ideas, and suggestions in this book are not intended as a substitute for professional advice. Before following any suggestions contained in this book, you should consult your personal physician or mental health professional. Neither the author nor the publisher shall be liable or responsible for any loss or damage allegedly arising as a consequence of your use or application of any information or suggestions in this book.

ISBN: 978-0-595-48522-2 (pbk)
ISBN: 978-0-595-60616-0 (ebk)

Printed in the United States of America

Contents

Introduction vii
Chapter I—Acceptance 1
Chapter II—Affection 10
Chapter III—Appreciation 21
Chapter IV—Approval 29
Chapter V—Attention 37
References 43

Introduction

I want to briefly discuss the reasons that I decided to write this book. Firstly, I realized that I was often having similar conversations with many of my patients about their relationships and their emotional needs. We spoke about their need to be loved and to feel appreciated, accepted, valued, and worthy of affection and attention from the significant people in their lives.

The more these conversations were repeated, the more I understood the significance of what we were discussing. When some patients would have difficulty articulating their emotional needs or feel guilty discussing them (as if they were being selfish for needing to be loved), I would try to justify and validate their thoughts and feelings by telling them that as humans we are social beings and by our very nature we need to be loved and appreciated by others.

The more my patients seemed to accept what I was sharing with them, the more I believed in it and was grateful to sense some relief in them. They seemed relieved in that even though their emotional needs may not have been met, at least someone understood what they were experiencing and that it was "okay" to want and need emotional fulfillment.

It was also rather gratifying and rewarding to be truly committed to what I was discussing with my patients. You see, throughout my academic and clinical training, I often felt like a sponge, needing to absorb, retain, and learn the theories, interventions, research, etc. It is a wonderful experience to arrive at a place in my career where I have come into my own theoretical orientation and style of counseling and to believe in and trust myself about what I have to share with others.

It is true what we are taught during our clinical training that our interactions with our patients will continually impact our own growth and development on both a personal and professional level. Well, the more I heard myself talk, the more I believed in and became passionate about what I was saying, and the more I felt compelled to put down my thoughts and ideas in writing to share with a larger group of people.

Secondly, I wanted to discuss acceptance, affection, appreciation, approval, and attention because of their integral connection to self-esteem, a concept that is often a core issue for many patients. Whether these patients are struggling with a mood or anxiety disorder, eating disorder, gender identity issue, or problematic relationship issues, many suffer with a negative self-concept. For some patients who do not feel good about themselves, this is difficult to admit much less explore within a therapeutic setting. Yet, for some patients who may be more insightful and introspective, they can articulate the reasons why they struggle with low self-esteem, often tracing the onset of their negative self-image to their early adolescence and high school years, family relationships, etc. However, they would often ask the question about how they could improve their current level of self-esteem. This led me to many questions about self-esteem such as: How is a healthy self-esteem attained? How does a person grow into an adult with a positive self-concept? What are the variables that effect self-esteem? Hence, the 5 "As."

I believe that self-esteem is profoundly affected by how individuals are treated by their significant caregivers and influenced by their early role models. If children are graced with the sense that they are accepted, approved of, and appreciated by others, and if they are endowed with loving affection and attention, they stand a better chance of feeling good about themselves by internalizing others' positive regard toward them. This self-regard, self-concept, sense of self, whatever the "self" prefix you understand best to describe how you think and feel about yourself, will likely impact the quality of the emotional connections that you develop with the significant people in your life, whether they are your spouse, children, siblings, friends, and/or co-workers.

I thought about the approach that I wanted to take toward this book. I wondered if I wanted to spend time doing research and citing others, or did I want to write more of a conversational book that would hopefully be "user-friendly." Well, I opted for the latter and would like to explore the concepts of the 5 "As" and emotional connections to others in closer detail.

I hope that you enjoy reading this book as much as I have enjoyed writing it and, I thank you for the attention that you have given to this endeavor.

I wish that your life is full of love and acceptance, affection, appreciation, approval, and attention!!

With warm regards,

Dyan Yacovelli, Psy.D.

Chapter I—Acceptance

The Random House Webster's College Dictionary defines the word "accept" as "to receive with approval or favor" (8). So how does this translate into the interpersonal dynamics between a parent and a child? How do parents express acceptance of their children and how does discipline factor into this?

Let's look at what it means to accept your child as he or she is, and then we will explore how this acceptance is expressed. To accept a child as s/he presents her/himself to the world is to embrace the whole individual of the child. A parent accepts both the physical nature as well as the personality of the child. For example, if little Johnnie is born with a large nose that happens to run in his DNA pool, as his parent, you accept it. You never tease him about it or complain to him that his nose is too big. Whatever your child's physical appearance is, for good or bad, it is no one's place to judge it. Unfortunately, there are plenty of people who will do that to your child, be it the bully at school or the next-door neighbor. Just as well, a parent should never tell his teenage daughter that, "If you could just lose 10 pounds, you'd be so much prettier." The rest of the world will likely send her that message. Parents need to accept their child 10 pounds overweight—end of story!!

If by acceptance, you think that I'm referring to some sort of positive, unconditional regard, you'd be correct. But don't misunderstand me, please. This doesn't mean that you allow your child to be undisciplined for the sake of parental acceptance. While accepting your child for the person s/he is becoming, you need to set guidelines and establish a value system that will direct your child's behaviors.

Most clinical psychologists will tell you that you should focus on the behavior and not the person when disciplining a child. For example, if your child behaves rudely toward a peer, you need to correct this behavior by focusing on the behavior and not by attacking your child. Now, you may think that this is just semantics or "psychobabble" because the behavior is coming from the person, so isn't it all the same? In theory, yes, but in practice, no. Let me give you an example.

If your child is playing with a friend and he exhibits rude behavior toward his friend, you should not tolerate this behavior. But you should also do not berate and degrade your child, especially in front of his peer. While some parents may think that embarrassing their children in front of peers serves as a good learning lesson in that the behavior would likely not be repeated, I would tend to disagree. Remember that the means may not always justify the end, with the end in this case being behavior modification. Still, some parents may argue that if a little bit of embarrassment modifies and corrects poor behavior, what's the harm?? Well, my point is just that. If there is harm caused by embarrassing your child, is there a different approach that will bring about the same behavior modification without any harm?

Let's work through a sample scenario. Your child is rude to his friend, and you lose your cool, yell at your child by telling him that, "He's being a rude, bad boy and if he doesn't knock it off right now, his friend will have to leave." Well, naturally he doesn't want to lose his playmate so he begrudgingly adapts his behavior. As a parent, you may think to yourself, "All is well, straightened out his attitude, huh!" However, what do you think years of this type of dynamic does to a child, i.e., being told that "you are bad" (not taking the time to differentiate between the behavior being bad and not "you" the person) and feeling embarrassed and ashamed in front of peers? Do you think that a child will start to internalize that he is bad along with all the baggage that is attached to the label of a "bad" person? Do you think that years of being made to feel embarrassed and ashamed will lower one's sense of worthiness, self-esteem, and self-confidence?

Here is an example of how the same rude behavior can be addressed. Take the time to sit down with your child and discuss the behavior by explaining why it was rude and inappropriate. Give an example of how the situation with the friend could have been handled. Ask your child to explain to you what you have discussed and how he would handle it better the next time he is playing with a friend. You could even role model a similar situation, giving your child the chance to practice how he should behave.

Listen, I am a firm believer in teaching a child moral behavior. A code of values and ethics is mandatory for a civil society. However, there is a big difference between disciplining your child and degrading him. DO discipline, DON'T disrespect. When a person (regardless of age, gender, race, creed, etc.) disrespects others, he disrespects himself. And remember, how you discipline your child is serving as a powerful role model for him. I cannot tell you how many times I have heard parents complain about their child's behavior or poor attitude. Unfortunately, most parents do not realize that this very behavior or attitude that they cannot tolerate is a mirror image of their own. Go figure!

I have worked many years with a gay and lesbian population, including gender identity disordered persons, and nothing tears at the core of these individuals more than not being accepted by their parents except, of course, an utter total and painful rejection, with many parents "disowning" their children. To be rejected and devalued by one's own parents, the very people who created you, can be devastating to an individual. If your parents don't accept and love the person that you are, how on earth are you to accept and love yourself when it has never been role modeled for you? Self-acceptance is key to having a sense of worthiness and an internal peace and happiness, without which life can be a tremendous struggle.

So how do parents express acceptance of their children to them? One thing I discovered during my years of counseling families and couples is the importance and impact of nonverbal communication. I will often ask a family member in a therapy session to explain the facial expression or other physical gesture (shrug of the shoulder, heavy sigh, roll of the eyes, etc.) that was made while another family member was speaking. The point is that we often communicate our thoughts and feelings quite effectively through nonverbal expression without being aware of it.

Parents need to be cognizant of their nonverbal communication with their children. I wonder sometimes what is more damaging to a child, the words, "I'm so disappointed in you" or the look of utter disappointment and disgust from a parent to a child. Now before you get defensive, let me explain. It is a natural reaction to feel disappointed in some of your child's behaviors. But, do you need to EXPRESS your disappointment so pointedly? Do you express your love and acceptance as eloquently?

Here is my concern: When you tell a child that s/he disappointed you, aren't you really saying that s/he "failed?" Do you really want to be held responsible for such a blow to your child's developing self-esteem? Isn't there a more nurturing way for you to express your thoughts and feelings without using the disappointing look or word? Can you be a more creative and encouraging parent?

A smile, a hug, and a three-word sentence such as, "Great job, son!" goes a long way in letting your child know that you accept him for the person that he is. But at an even more basic level, when you interact with your child, you should look at him. Don't be reading the newspaper or sorting the mail. Let your child know that you are interested in him by showing your interest. You should express some genuine enthusiasm and excitement toward your child and spend some quality time with him that doesn't always involve academics or sports. More on the topic of attention in a later chapter.

Let's explore acceptance between spouses/partners. As humans we are all flawed, and we all have our warts, sort of speak. And this is a good thing because it's real, it's actual, and it just might keep us safe from trying to be "perfect." We need to be able to accept our own flaws as well as those flaws of our partner. Trust me, I have witnessed young adolescents as well as younger and older adults whose strivings for perfectionism just about impair their ability to live their life let alone enjoy it. So what is the point in being just "right" if you can't feel good about yourself and your life?

One common mistake that many couples make (especially after they are married) is that they try to change their mates into the person that they want them to be. Let me give you an example. Often one person within the couple takes on the financial management tasks. This may happen for a myriad of reasons. Perhaps one is a better money manager or doesn't work outside the home and has more time for such tasks. A problem arises when the mate responsible for financial tasks wants help or wants to delegate the complete set of tasks to the other mate, who may not be good at paying bills in a timely fashion. Thus, the battle begins to convert a fiscally irresponsible person into a certified public accountant.

If the trait that you are trying to change is an inherent personality trait, it just may not be susceptible to change, and you will likely spend the majority of your togetherness fighting a losing battle. Wouldn't it be easier and more peaceful just to accept each other for the negative and positive traits that you both have? And, in order to do this it is very important that you know each other quite well prior to making a serious, long-term commitment. You need to understand what traits you can accept and what ones you cannot accept in a mate. And, in order to have a clear understanding of what you can and cannot tolerate, it is necessary that you know yourself well so that you have an awareness of what you want and need in a life partner.

So if you cannot tolerate a person who is slovenly, you need to make sure that your life partner is a neat person. If someone has racial or gay biases and you cannot stand these traits, it is best that you learn this about the person. It takes time to truly and intimately know another person. I am amazed when I hear about people marrying after only three to six months of knowing each other. This is not to say that they will not have a long and loving relationship. It's just that they still have so much to discover about each other's character and personality. It is best to take your time and make a commitment when you feel confident and sure about your choice in a mate.

Let me differentiate between trying to change your mate's traits and appropriate compromise. The willingness to compromise depends not only on how ingrained these traits are but on how open the person is on working toward a compromise. Being able to compromise is a way to show your consideration and thoughtfulness toward your mate as well as maintain a peaceful coexistence.

Let's explore an example of a successful compromise between mates. Some customary habits may be more susceptible to change than innate traits. Examples include domestic and household habits such as putting down the toilet seat, not using the bedroom floor as your personal hamper, etc. Personality traits may not be so open to adjustment. For example, if you are with a partner who has difficulty expressing his emotions or is not verbally or physically affectionate toward you and you enjoy emotional and physical intimacy, you have a serious problem.

Hence, my point about knowing well what you need in a mate and selecting a mate who meets your needs. It is not wise to think that you will be able to change him/her. Now, don't get me wrong, couple therapy may help with many problematic issues. However, BOTH parties need to be open to the experience and be willing to make an effort to "adjust, progress, and grow" in the same direction.

I tell many of my patients that I don't have a magic wand and if they are seeking real change, then they must make the effort to bring about the change. It is quite rewarding to hear a couple say that they have seen positive progress and growth in their relationship, and that they recognize that they communicate with each other more effectively with a greater level of understanding and acceptance.

Acceptance of your children, spouse, and partner helps to create an environment wherein one can feel loved for who s/he is, and this helps in turn for one to better accept oneself, flaws and all. I also believe that it is equally important that we accept our parents as they are, for all the good as well as the bad. I have seen many adults too invested in the emotions of anger and sadness from not being able to accept the parent(s) that reared them. Well, you know that old saying, "You can't choose your relatives."

Let me give a very common example of a parent who is hard to accept: the emotionally unavailable parent who cannot give verbal affirmations or physical affection to his/her children. As a young person being raised by this type of parent, it is difficult to understand that the parent's emotional unavailability has nothing to do with you and everything to do with the parent's upbringing and life experiences.

A child will think that a parent's inability to express his/her love and affection to the child is due to the fact that the child is unworthy of love. Yet, a child will struggle for the majority of his/her childhood and adolescent years to do everything in his/her power to receive the love and acceptance that is needed from the parent. This dynamic often leads to the child feeling unloved, unwanted, and not valued. What do you think the effect of these feelings is on this child's sense of self?

A common defense mechanism against the hurt and sadness that results from not feeling loved by an emotionally absent parent is withdrawal and anger. It is a way to protect oneself from the profound pain and sense of rejection. Anger often masks hurt because it is the safer emotion to express in that it makes one feel less vulnerable. I see this often within problematic family dynamics when the parents' primary complaint about their teenager is the intense rage that s/he displays. What they don't grasp is that there is likely sadness and hurt behind the rage.

Although there is justification for the emotions of anger, hurt, and sadness toward a parent who was not capable of meeting a child's emotional needs, if these emotions carry into adulthood, they could very likely interfere with healthy emotional development and growth as well as the ability to have trusting and loving relationships with others. Defense mechanisms utilized in one's upbringing to help cope with an unloving, if not hostile, family environment can be viewed as adaptive functioning in that they helped individuals deal with their family and social environment. However, the very same defense mechanisms utilized in adulthood may in fact become maladaptive when they interfere with the ability to create and maintain loving and supportive relationships with others. Hence, my point about accepting your parents for whom they are, including their deficits, and moving forward in a more positive direction with your life.

The first step in accepting your parents is an understanding that their behavior toward their children is more reflective of the type of person that they are and is not an indicator of your worth as a person. It may also be helpful to understand your parent's family background and upbringing and the significant influences that impacted their parenting skills and behaviors. Understanding is often the key to acceptance because when you understand other persons, you may be more empathic and compassionate toward them. Having an understanding and compassionate mindset is much more positive than an angry and resentful mindset. And, a more positive mindset will hopefully lead to acceptance.

Accepting persons for who they are does not mean that you have to agree with them or even like their views, beliefs, traits, etc. Acceptance will hopefully benefit you by leading to a sense of inner peace, with you being less angry with and bitter toward others. A corollary of accepting others "AS IS" is that it helps facilitate the setting of appropriate boundaries, i.e., "They are them, but I am me, and we can be related yet we can also be very different from each other." When you are able to view yourself as a separate individual from your problematic family of origin, you have a better chance of not internalizing the negative experiences and your parent's deficits as being reflective of your worthiness as a human being. Therefore, you have a choice in that even though you recognize that you stem from problematic (e.g., unloving, unaffectionate, etc.) roots, that your life and your relationships don't have to be problematic, and that you can in fact work toward the goal of having a fulfilling emotional life as an adult.

I believe that many of us fantasize about having the ideal parents and family life and what we would like to have experienced during our growing years. Well, you know that old saying about, "Accepting the cards that you are dealt." On a positive note, many of us take our upbringing deficits and make sure not to repeat them with our own children. I especially see this tendency in regard to the issue of affection. And, I am delighted to report that I have heard many male patients state that they make an effort to show affection to their children, having known what it feels like to crave the acceptance and affection of their own parent only to be left wanting and needing. So what is affection and how does it impact emotional fulfillment?

Chapter II—Affection

The Random House Webster's College Dictionary defines the word "affection" as "fond attachment, devotion, or love; an emotion, feeling, sentiment." This is the noun description of affection. The adjective description of being affectionate is "showing affection or love; fondly tender, loving; having a great affection or love" (23). Now that we have an understanding of what affection is, I would like to explore the verb form of affection. How does affection appear as an action? You know that old adage, "Put you money where your mouth is" (or something to that effect). In other words, "Mean what you say, and say what you mean." So if a person describes himself as affectionate, how does this translate into actions?

How do we express affection for each other? How do parents show devotion, love, and a fond tenderness toward their children? How do partners/spouses express love and affection toward each other? And, what are the myriad ways of showing affection, such as verbal communication, nonverbal communication (physical gestures of hugs and caresses, handholding, etc.), doing things for each other (such as making a meal for your mate), gift buying, enjoying social activities with each other, etc.

Let's first explore how parents express affection to their children. Much to my dismay, many of the adolescent female patients that I have treated over the years who have had problematic relationships with their parents were desperately seeking acceptance and approval from them. And, what better way to feel a sense of acceptance and approval from parents than when they show their love through different forms of affection.

Yet, many of these young female patients had parents, especially dads, who never hugged them. I remember one 15-year-old female patient muttering through tears that the only relationship she had with her dad was when he was yelling at her. Her mother sat there appearing in shock at her daughter's statement. I asked her what she thought about what her daughter had just said and she replied, "She's right. I never realized that he doesn't interact much with her except to yell at her." This is an example of what continues to amaze me about the therapeutic experience because people live their lives day in and day out without taking a moment to reflect upon their lives and their relationships. It often takes some sort of a crisis such as an eating disorder, chemical substance abuse, self-mutilation, etc. and a trip to a physician's, psychiatrist's, or psychologist's office to realize the deficits, if not dysfunctions, within a family unit.

I have also had many dads tell me that, "I am just not comfortable hugging my children regardless of their gender or age. And, furthermore, I was never hugged as a child and I turned out just fine." Oh, really?!? Some people think that if they grow up and become law-abiding citizens and hard-working persons, that they are "good parents." Well, they may be good providers but are they "good-enough" parents? If so, why are their daughters starving themselves or slicing up their bodies? Listen, there are many factors that influence an adolescent's behavior and this conversation isn't meant to blame parents, but we do need to be honest and look at whether or not parents are being affectionate toward their children and are meeting their emotional needs as well as what the ramifications may be on a child who is starving for affection from a parent.

Let's start by exploring the basics of physical displays of affection. Some of the most common forms of physical affection are hugging and embracing each other. Another common form is kissing each other. Parents will often hug and kiss their children hello and goodbye each day. It is important to note that the physical displays from parents to their children will likely have an impact on how they grow up and express themselves as affectionate adults. Let me share an interesting account from a female patient.

This patient came from a family whose father was emotionally absent and whose mother had more of a despotic nature than that of a loving, nurturing mother. Needless to say, this patient was reared in an inattentive and unaffectionate family. However, she was very close to one of her aunts, who was like a surrogate mother to her. Her aunt was a very loving and affectionate person. When the patient was in her late 20s, she went on a road-trip vacation with her family and her aunt's family. She decided to return home earlier than her family so her parents and aunt and uncle took her to the airport. As customary practice, her aunt and uncle embraced her as they said their goodbyes. Upon their return from the vacation, the patient's mother commented to her in a 'typical condescending and judgmental tone,' "That's pretty good, at the airport you hugged your aunt and uncle goodbye but not your own parents!" The patient's response to her mother was, "No, mom, you're mistaken, aunt and uncle hugged me goodbye." The patient further explained that what was even sadder about this incident was that her mother likely didn't feel genuinely hurt that she wasn't hugged by her daughter. It was more of an issue of embarrassment in front of the aunt and uncle or one of jealousy in that the daughter seemed to prefer the aunt as a maternal figure.

This incident reminds me of a song by Harry Chapin entitled "Cat's In the Cradle." The song is about the 'little boy blue and the man in the moon.' The central theme of the song is that the father is too busy to spend time with his son during his growing years. Once the son becomes a man and has his own family and busy life, the dad reaches out and wants to spend more time with his son. Well, the son is too busy and the father realizes, "Ah, my son has grown up just like me." Well, you know that old saying, "You reap what you sow!"

So what other ways can parents show affection toward their children other than through physical touch? Let's explore some other nonverbal forms of expressing affection toward your children. How about a basic facial gesture such as a smile? We likely underestimate the meaning and power of a simple, nonverbal gesture such as a smile.

As an example, let's take a daily routine interchange between a parent and a child when the parent picks up the child from school. The parent spots his child in the emerging crowd of youngsters fleeing school and waves and gives a big smile to him/her. What message do you think is being sent by that smile? Perhaps one that says, "Hey, I'm excited to see you." And, how do you think that this message is internalized by the child? Perhaps s/he is getting the sense that they must be a person of value, one that is appreciated and loved by the parent.

Now, if all this can be accomplished by a smile, just imagine how powerful verbal communication can be. There are endless ways that words can express affection from a parent to a child. The most direct path would be telling your children that you love them. However, all positive and affirming words to your children deliver the message that you have a loving and warm affection for them.

What are some other ways to express affection for your children? Well, we can't overlook the slippery slope of gift buying. Although it is very natural for parents to want to buy things for their children, it is a slippery slope because it should not be a gesture that replaces other forms of needed affection. Unfortunately, many parents who are not comfortable with direct, personal expressions of affection toward their children through physical and verbal means try to compensate by buying material items for their children. All this does is ease the guilt of a parent while likely spoiling a child who becomes rich in goods and poor in love. In addition, some of us may confuse material wealth and comfort with emotional wealth and comfort. Many times kids being raised in the projects are better loved than those raised by nannies.

Another way of expressing affection is by doing deeds for your children. Naturally, as a parent it is your duty to do certain tasks such as provide for your children's basic needs of food, clothing, shelter, education, safety, and security. And, although it doesn't hurt to remind your children that part of the reason that you work to earn an income is to provide for their needs, you don't want to overdo it. Here's an example from a 15-year-old patient. She reported that she felt like a "burden" to her parents because her mom would complain daily about the need to work two jobs to put food on the table. Do you think that feeling like a "burden" on her parents will affect her sense of worth and self-value, which in turn will likely affect her sense of self-esteem? Do you think that I'm being dramatic for the sense of being dramatic? I wish I was. No, in fact, this is the plain truth. If parents speak words and act in such a manner that their children feel unloved and unwanted, it will have a negative impact on them. Some parents simply don't realize the power of their words and behaviors.

Other deeds that are above and beyond those expected by parents that express affection to a child range from participating in social activities with them, reading with them, etc. The list is endless. Parents doing anything positive for and with a child, regardless of the exact deed, sends the message that they are interested in them, that they love them, and that they have a deep affection for them.

An important way to show affection to your children is by spending "quality" time with them. The emphasis is on quality, which doesn't mean that you're in one room of the house paying bills while your child is in another room playing video games. Even if it's a 15–30 minute walk after dinner during which you talk about each other's day, that is quality time. Too often I have spoken with teenagers who did not know what their parents' occupation was. And, why do you think that is so? It is because some parents and children don't talk to each other as often as they should. So, my advice to parents is to spend time with your children, look into each other's eyes and listen when you speak to one another, and above all else, SMILE☺.

Now, let's explore how affection is expressed between spouses/partners. Many of the interchanges of affection between a parent and a child are similar to that between spouses/partners. There are the non-verbal, physical gestures that express affection such as embracing each other before leaving the house for work as well as when returning home from work. Spouses/partners often enjoy handholding and walking arm-in-arm as other forms of physical expression.

Sexual relations are another expression of physical affection between mates. However, this is sometimes a problematic area when there is a disparity between sexual drives. Regardless of the length of a relationship, many couples are uncomfortable having an open and direct conversation about their sexual relationship. I try to understand that many people are just "naturally" embarrassed by such a personal topic. But, I usually always conclude with this thought, "Wait a minute, you can 'do it' but you can't talk about it." Go figure!! However, there are many couples that enjoy a loving and fulfilling sexual relationship, giving them another form for expressing their feelings for one another.

I think that it is important to understand that there are differences between physical, sexual, and emotional intimacy even though they are all forms of expressing affection toward your mate. So let's explore these different types of intimacies.

I had a male patient who told me that his wife complained to him that they had no emotional intimacy. He then said that he had no idea what she was talking about because he didn't know what emotional intimacy was and asked if I could explain it to him. I told him that the first step to having emotional intimacy with your partner was to have an awareness of your emotions. It is a simple concept yet an important one, i.e., that awareness is key to a deeper understanding of many of the important issues we encounter in our life. Many of us live our daily lives thinking and feeling full throttle, but we often do not take the time to reflect upon our thoughts and feelings let alone discuss them with our life partner.

It continues to amaze me when I ask patients what they are feeling, and they look at me as if I'm speaking a foreign language. I often have to give them a multiple-choice selection from which to identify their emotion, e.g., "Well, did that make you feel sad, angry, afraid, or did you feel a mixture of emotions?" It is as if reflecting on our thoughts and feelings and our emotional needs is a luxury that not many of us can afford. I think that it is a luxury we can't afford to ignore if we are seeking emotional fulfillment.

So in reviewing the first step of emotional intimacy, we need to experience emotions and be aware of what they are. The second step is to be willing and able to share these emotions with one's partner. As I explained to my male patient (who was a very stereotypical law enforcement man and was uncomfortable with therapy lest it would emasculate him), sharing emotions with your partner is not limited to just the emotions between you and your partner. For example, you can have an emotional reaction to a story that you hear on the news and discuss your thoughts and feelings with your partner.

The natural consequence of opening up yourself and sharing your thoughts and emotions with your mate is the creation of a bond and a closeness: a real, authentic, intimate connection. As a result of this bond and connection, a level of intimacy is established between partners, allowing them to derive the sweetest sensation of incredible warmth and comfort from each other. I think one of the greatest feelings in the world is when your partner knows you very well, and you get the sense of truly being understood by and connected to another human being.

Now, let me clarify the difference between emotional intimacy and physical/sexual intimacy. While sexual intimacy may in fact enhance a sense of emotional closeness, it does not take the place of it. The same applies to physical intimacy such as hugging, handholding, etc. While physical acts of affection will likely impact a sense of emotional closeness between partners, it doesn't take the place of emotional intimacy. So you may be wondering then how exactly is emotional intimacy established: it is mostly attained through verbal communication.

I tend to think that at the base of emotional closeness is a willingness to open up and verbally communicate with one's partner while any warm and affectionate nonverbal communication is "icing on the cake." This explains why I have heard many patients say that they have satisfying sexual relationships with their mates and that their mates are physically affectionate toward them, but "… something's missing!" and they don't know what it is.

Just like physical and sexual intimacy can enhance emotional intimacy between partners, the opposite is true, with emotional intimacy making physical and sexual intimacy between partners more satisfying and rewarding. The tricky thing about these various intimacies between partners is that they don't happen automatically when people fall in love. Intimacy and its rewards take an awareness: an awareness of one's own needs and the gusto to attain the desired relationship with your mate. Once you attain it, the next feat is to maintain a fulfilling level of intimacy with your mate.

In order to have a level of emotional intimacy, one must be willing to open up oneself to his/her mate. Well, this takes risks and a willingness to make oneself vulnerable to another person. Why vulnerable? Well, when we totally expose our real inner selves, for good or bad, we risk disapproval and rejection. But, unfortunately, this is how intimacy works. Or put another way, the flip side of the emotional intimacy coin is vulnerability, and you can't have one without the other. An analogy would be that of a person who never felt the pure joy of true love because he was so afraid of opening his heart to the experience for fear of the pain that would be caused by the love being lost. Well, I'm sure you have heard the saying, "Better to have loved and lost then to never have loved at all."

I tend to view many aspects of life either on a continuum or by using the coin analogy, wherein there is often a positive and negative flip side. Whether it's from the continuum or coin perspective, as long as you strive for some sort of reasonable balance, you should remain relatively emotionally stable and healthy, you know, "Everything in moderation."

Let me give an example of the continuum perspective by using the trait of perfectionism. Perfectionism is a trait that can make your approach to life either adaptive or maladaptive depending where one is rated on a continuum scale. For example, on a scale from 1–10 (with ten being the highest), if a patient rates his perfectionistic strivings at a 10, this is likely a person struggling with symptoms of a mood and/or anxiety disorder. These are persons who are likely very tense about life being just so perfect that the slightest event that skews the ideal can really wreck havoc in their world. I often think of these people as wound-up tops that are wrapped so tightly, never allowing them to spin out and enjoy the ride of life. So this is an example of how being on the wrong end of the continuum could be maladaptive. Being on the other end of the continuum may not be too adaptive, either. Someone who rates himself on the scale of perfectionistic strivings as a 1 or 2 may be a person who is lacking in motivation and ambition or is indolent, unproductive, and cares very little about personal strivings and achievement.

I tend to think that a rating somewhere in the middle of the scale, ranging perhaps from 4–8, is likely the most adaptive in perfectionistic traits. The tricky thing about viewing mental health traits on a continuum is that one step to the right might make your interaction with the world adaptive while one step to the left, maladaptive. You know that other old saying, "There's a fine line between love and hate." Well, sometimes there is a very fine line between mental health and mental chaos.

Perhaps the most important question to address is why many of us think that we have to be perfect. Hey, I'd be the first to admit that some perfectionistic strivings motivate one to work toward and achieve personal goals. But what is at the core of one's striving to be perfect? Why do we care so darn much about this ideal of what we think we should be? I'll tell you why, it is because we think that if we are "just right" then we will get all the love, attention, and affection that we need. Well, the joke's on us, because this is not true at all.

Let's take an example of a population that is riddled with obsessive/compulsive perfectionistic strivings: bulimic teenagers. A bulimic teen believes that if her body is "just perfect" that she'll get that emotionally elusive father of hers to give her the acceptance, affection, appreciation, approval, and attention that she is so desperately longing to have. Unfortunately, her bout with bulimia will likely not fill the emotional void that is reserved for paternal attachment and recognition. Thus, she will continue to struggle with trying to nourish her emotional needs with food until some sort of effective mental health intervention helps her work through and resolve these issues. In regard to emotional eating, I recall reading one time a very powerful point that utilizing a tangible item, such as food, to satisfy an intangible need, such as the need for love and affection, will simply not work, with the person being physically filled to capacity while the emotional hunger continues.

Whether the relationship is one between spouses or a parent and a child, we all need a sense of an intimate connection to other human beings. We need to feel comfortable being ourselves and being accepted by others for who we are and not some ideal or rigid, perfected model of who we and/or others think that we should be. We could incapacitate ourselves with the pressure that we put on us to be "perfect," and in so doing, we limit the joy and pleasure of simply relaxing and participating in our lives.

In addition to the verbal and nonverbal forms of affection that help create intimate connections with our mates, other ways of expressing affection include spending quality time with each other as well as doing things for one another. I must confess that nothing would make my heart swoon more than any bunch of flowers or expensive gift then when the mate in my life would offer to make me a cup of tea or voluntarily massage my feet. Those are real gifts!!

Spending quality time together doesn't necessarily mean that the two of you need to do everything with each other. If she wants to spend Saturday morning golfing with some friends while he prefers to remain at home and do landscaping tasks (or vice versa), that's perfectly acceptable. You can both have different interests and hobbies. What is important is that you spend enough time with each other that is satisfying to both of you.

Some problems that I have seen between partners occur when one has a multitude of outside interests or hobbies and the other does not. The problem arises when the one without hobbies becomes too demanding and requests that the other reduce the hobbies/activities so that they can spend more time with each other. This is another example of getting to know each other well prior to making a long-term commitment. If you are a homebody and prefer to cook, garden, and entertain at home on weekends but your mate is a social butterfly and prefers going out every night of the weekend, this could be a problem. Even something as basic as opposite work schedules, with him being a night owl while she may be a morning person, could interfere with spending quality time with each other.

When people speak about being compatible with their mates, they often discuss different variables of compatibility such as intellectual, emotional, physical/sexual attraction, spiritual, and social compatibility. However, I think that the issue of social compatibility isn't given the same attention and focus that the other variables are given until there is a problem. An example of this type of problem usually presents itself in a conjoint therapy session as such: "She knew when we got married that I played softball two nights of the week. Now, all of a sudden, she wants me to stop playing so that I can stay home with her." Hence, make sure that you are socially compatible since this is an important aspect of a healthy and balanced relationship.

A great deal of affection for your mate can be displayed in numerous ways. However, you need to have the ability and willingness to show your affection and gratitude to your mate. This leads to the next aspect of appreciation. How do we show appreciation for one another and what effect does this have on our emotional connectedness to others?

Chapter III—Appreciation

I'll keep this definition simple. The Random House Webster's College Dictionary defines appreciation as "gratitude; thankful recognition" (68). How do parents show gratitude and thankful recognition of their children to them? I must say that nothing gets my goat more than when parents don't understand the concept of showing appreciation for their children.

It has been my observation that many parents did not choose to have children for the pure sake of loving and nurturing them let alone enjoying their company. Many people have children for the following reasons:

1. It is the thing to do, i.e., grow up, get a job, get married, and raise a family. It is the civilized way, isn't it? It doesn't require much thought let alone much rhyme or reason. It's been said that, "You need a license to drive a car but not to raise children!;"

2. To create an extension of themselves and their family heritage. This isn't necessarily a bad motive for having children except when parents regard their children as objects of possession and not individuals entitled to their own separate and distinct personalities and lives;

3. To have someone to love, especially for a person who desires a strong sense of social cohesiveness that stems from a loving and supportive family; and

4. Ooops, the unplanned pregnancy that too often results in an unwanted child. Imagine the uphill battle for the child who is reared by a parent that regrets his very existence.

On a positive note, many people have children for the right reasons. But even if their motives are appropriate, do parents really understand the need to appreciate their offspring? Let's examine an act of appreciation at its most basic level.

What is a customary way of letting people know that you are grateful to them for whatever the reason may be? A simple "thank you" usually does the trick. Now, I can already hear some parents' uproar, "Why should I say thank you to my kids for doing what is expected of them?" Well, first of all, behavior research will substantiate that positive behavior will likely be repeated if it is reinforced. So when your children get good grades in school and complete their chores without constantly being reminded, wouldn't it be nice to let them know that you appreciate all that they do. I would venture to guess that not many parents have any qualms about letting their children know when they do things that are not appreciated.

And, let's not forget the first two "As" of Acceptance and Affection, which are sure-fire ways of letting your child know that s/he is appreciated. Throughout my years that I have had the pleasure and honor (pleasure because I enjoy my work and honor because people trust me enough to open up and share their very personal issues) of participating in family therapy sessions, the best relationships between parents and their children were those wherein the parents had a genuine interest in their children as well as an appreciation for them.

However, if I'm seeing a family because of problematic issues and relationships between parents and the children, there often is a lack of appreciation from the parent toward the child. In fact, there is usually an itemized list from the parent of all that is wrong with the child. Here's a typical therapeutic scenario: Both mom and dad bring in their 15-year-old daughter with this complaint list:

1. She's angry all the time;
2. She refuses to eat;
3. She's rude to her siblings;

4. Her grades have dropped dramatically, etc., etc., etc.

And, they go on and give a short family history, stating that "We are good parents and there is nothing wrong with our other two children, who are great athletes and students, so if you could just fix what's wrong with this daughter, all will be right with our family." Oh, really, want to bet?!? Gosh, if I had a dollar or two for every parent who blamed their children for their problems, I'd have no mortgage payment!!

Look, we all do things that might not always be appreciated by those closest to us, but when we do rock the boat and make waves, it's as if we have no appreciable value. And, this is often the perception of a frustrated parent. Well, what do you think the effect is on the child who is having some difficulty and isn't appreciated at all by the parents? Do you think there's much incentive to improve upon the current problematic situation, especially when the child feels like a total failure and disappointment to the parents?

Sometimes when a family therapy session gets so dark and gloomy, with mom trying to outdo dad's complaint list (which is one of the reasons I often meet with the parents before their child joins us in the initial session), I'll just have to interject and ask them to tell me a couple of positive traits about their child. The length of time that it takes for them to recite one is usually indicative of just how dire the situation may be.

The parents who do have a genuine liking and appreciation for their child can easily display it be just simply showing an interest in their child. I saw a mother and her 17-year-old daughter for family therapy, and the mother had a loving warmth and regard toward her daughter, who she intently listened to and did not interrupt when she spoke. The mom treated her daughter as a person that she knew well and about whom she truly cared. I remember feeling so touched by their affection and appreciation for each other. I then felt sadly that this relationship wasn't the norm that I encountered. But, you must remember that I have a skewed view, with many loving and nurturing families not in need of therapeutic intervention.

Listen, I understand that it is hard to show appreciation to your children when they are frustrating you with their behaviors. But these problems don't get any better by showing a total depreciation for your child. When this happens, a total disregard and disrespect is not far behind, and then these feelings need to be dealt with in therapy in addition to the initial presenting problems. An example of this would be when a parent curses at a child in a therapy session or doesn't like what the child is saying (which usually is an appropriate topic to discuss) and will order the child to be quiet. Well, naturally, you can see that we have to deal with the issue of appropriate and effective communication as well as the other critical issues that brought them into therapy.

In addition to showing your child thankful recognition and gratitude, parents should also truly feel a sense of appreciation for their child. If parents can do this, then it will be easy to put their child's emotional needs before their own. You see, I believe that it is the parents' duty and obligation to put the emotional needs of their children first. This may not always be an easy thing to do. But, you know what, parents are the grownups so they need to act like grownups. Another thing that gets my goat is when adolescents act more responsible and mature than the parents.

Let me give you an example of a common instance when a parent puts his or her needs above the child's needs. When there is a bitter divorce in a family, there is often a bitter ex-husband or ex-wife who hurt the children by saying negative things about the other parent. If parents truly appreciated their children and cared about their emotional well-being, they would behave in a manner that showed it. They don't vent their anger, frustration, resentment, etc. about the ex-spouse to relieve their emotional angst at the expense of their children. Here is a horrid example. I had a 14-year-old patient tell me that when her dad and step-mom were breaking up, the step-mom called her and 'ranted and raved' about how, "No good her father was, he was back to his old ways of drinking, couldn't be trusted, ..." I just looked at my patient in shock that an adult would do this to a 14-year-old adolescent. She read my facial expression accurately and replied, "Yeah, can you believe she said that to his daughter." The 14-year-old had more sense than the adult!

So, you see, although the concept of appreciation seems very basic, there's more to it than just how you show regard toward your child. It is about a mental mindset, as well. Sometimes, the simplest ideas, such as appreciation, can also be the most profound. Let's now explore the art of appreciation between spouses/partners.

One of the chief complaints that I hear from some female patients is the hurt, sadness, anger, resentment, disappointment, etc. that they feel from a lack of being appreciated by the significant persons in their lives. Most of these women have a multitude of roles, i.e., they are wives, mothers, daughters, sisters, grandmothers, employees, etc. Interestingly, if these women sensed a lack of appreciation from others in each role that they had, then it was likely due to an inherent personality trait and/or psychological/emotional issue. Unlike if a patient felt unappreciated by her boss but very valued by others in her life, then it was likely due to her boss's personality or the work situation.

But if you find yourself wanting of appreciation by most loved ones in your life, then I think it is important to explore how you and your history might contribute to this interpersonal dynamic. Let's take an example of a patient that I once treated. She struggled with a myriad of emotions due to a sense of not feeling appreciated as a wife, mother, grandmother, sister, daughter, and employee. It's as if she had this big hole in her that she couldn't fill with emotional connectedness to others so she tried to fill it with food and alcohol. Needless to say, self-medicating didn't work, and in fact, it made matters worse, so she tried individual and marital therapy.

Therapy helped her to recognize that she suffered with a very low self-esteem and negative sense of self-worth. She traced these issues to her childhood and adolescence, during which she was raised by an alcoholic, depressed mother and a verbally abusive father, who berated her whenever he chose to speak to her. To try to compensate for her upbringing and lack of self-worth, she became a bit of an overachiever, needing to be the best mother, wife, employee, etc. Her intention was to be the best at whatever the endeavor was so that she could get the thankful recognition and gratitude that she had been seeking her entire life.

Unfortunately, no matter what others did to show their appreciation of her, it was never enough to satisfy her needs. You've heard it said that, "You have to first love yourself before you allow others to love you." Well, until this patient was able to feel a sense of appreciation and value for herself, it was hard for her to find herself worthy of others' appreciation for her.

You might be thinking, "Yeah, easier said than done," and you'd be right. It is hard to change a negative self-image into a positive one, but it can be done. Recognizing that a core issue is low self-esteem and a lack of appreciation for your own self is only the first step. The rest of the work involves fixing the problem. I had a long-term patient who was rather insightful and was able to recognize that her low self-esteem was a factor in her dysfunctional relationships wherein she often was the victim. She firmly stated during one session the following, "I understand my problem as well as its origin, so how do I improve upon my self-esteem and feel better about myself?" Good question, huh?!?

Well, here is a synopsis of my reply. Firstly, I positively reinforced her ability to honestly look at herself and understand what her issues were. And, this wasn't just some rote psychobabble feedback. I truly believe that recognition and understanding of a problematic issue are fundamental aspects of the healing process. Also, when people are feeling down about themselves, it doesn't hurt to say something positive about them. But, more importantly, this positive affirmation within the therapeutic alliance may be key to psychological growth and progress, which I will elaborate on later.

Secondly, I explained to the patient (who was in her mid-40s) that she has lived the majority of her life struggling with low self-esteem issues, and that it wasn't something that can be fixed overnight. She needed to be patient and actively work on improving this condition and, that it might take some time until she feels better. Remember, I don't have a magic wand (wish I did), and there isn't a medication on the market that helps specifically elevate self-esteem (wish there was).

In terms of dealing with low self-esteem, I tend to take a direct, somewhat cognitive-behavioral approach. I believe that our perceptions (distorted ones as well as accurate ones) directly influence our thoughts and feelings, which in turn impact our behaviors. Some cognitive-behavioral techniques include challenging the distorted perceptions and thus changing one's thoughts, feelings, and behaviors to more positive and proactive ones. I might ask patients to make a realistic list itemizing all the traits that they would like to change about themselves so that they could feel better about the person that they are. I emphasize "realistic" in that a 5'2" patient shouldn't be wasting her wish list on wanting to be 5'10" in height. Just isn't going to happen!

Once this list is presented, we review it and explore strategies that are practical. For example, if a patient regrets never having received a college education and feels "less than" many others in her social network including her spouse, neighbors, co-workers, siblings, etc. because of her lack of education, we explore the possibility of her taking some college classes. Listen, this doesn't necessarily mean that she'll complete a bachelor's or master's degree and start a new career as a result (although this could happen). The point is that if she took a couple of classes and completed them successfully and felt better about herself, then a therapeutic goal was accomplished. This is an example of how therapy and its goals can take some time to achieve.

Overcoming strife through life experiences and becoming stronger, more competent, and more empowered can also contribute to a sense of confidence that in turn can help increase one's level of self-esteem and belief in oneself. There is nothing I enjoy hearing more then when a patient says something to the effect of, "A year ago I would have handled this situation the old way. Now, I feel stronger and can deal with this matter more effectively." Even this statement is positively reinforcing to the patient because hearing oneself admit accomplishments is a powerful tool that leads to feeling better about oneself.

Another more subtle way of how one's level of self-esteem and self-appreciation increases over time is through a "corrective therapeutic experience." Simply put, the positive reflections and affirmations made by the therapist (who is often viewed as the surrogate parent) are internalized by the patient. The stronger the empathic and genuine bond is between the patient and the therapist, the better likelihood of this process occurring. When the patient has a positive regard and respect for the therapist, the subconscious may work as such: "I like this person and s/he likes me. Well, then, I must be worth liking." Once again, the simplest of processes can also have the most profound effects.

Once a person has attained a level of appreciation for oneself, it is much easier to take in the appreciation of others as well as display appreciation toward others. Appreciation between spouses and partners can be displayed in many ways similar to that of affection. There are verbal and nonverbal ways of expressing one's appreciation. Sometimes just a gentle caress on the shoulder can be a powerful manifestation of valuing someone. Spending quality time with your mate and doing special things for each other are all ways and opportunities to show gratitude and recognition for that other person's presence in your life.

Chapter IV—Approval

The Random House Webster's College Dictionary defines approval as "the act of speaking or thinking favorably of; to find to be acceptable" (68). As you can see, there is an overlap between acceptance and approval, which is why as children and adolescents (and often as adults, too) we seek both the acceptance and approval of our parents. We also may seek the approval of other authority figures such as teachers, employers, etc.

Why is it that we need a sense of approval from others? Why isn't it something that we innately have? Why do we depend on others for a sense of validation? I think that it is because of our social need for interaction with others. We don't exist in a vacuum and as such, our existence is intermingled and influenced by other social beings. I also think that seeking approval of one's parents is reflective of our social structure.

As family therapy models will demonstrate, a healthy family structure is one wherein mom and dad (or the two parents) are a unified dyad at the top of the hierarchical structure with well-defined boundaries as well as a well-defined power structure. The parents are in charge and they set up the rules by which the children are expected to behave. Naturally, if the children act in accordance to the standards that are set by the parents, they receive approval and vice versa, i.e., when the children misbehave, they receive disapproval from their parents.

This could be another slippery slope as addressed in the chapter about Acceptance. Naturally, it is the parents' responsibility to discipline their children when they do not approve of their behaviors. But sometimes there is a fine line between disciplining and degrading your children. A parent can mete out discipline without decimating the child.

What makes this issue such a delicate one is just this: if discipline of a child is handled appropriately, the child instinctively feels that the approval of the parent is at risk and will often modify the behavior so as to maintain the approval and acceptance of the parent. However, if the parent vilifies the child above and beyond what is appropriate for the offensive behavior, the child will likely experience an overwhelming sense of rejection and disapproval by the parent that s/he is left without much incentive for behavior modification. Remember the importance of focusing on the behavior without judging the individual as "all evil." Now, that may seem like an exaggeration, but how many times have you been in a store and observed a parent berating a child that seemed to be a bit "extreme" if not borderline verbally abusive.

Listen, even parents are entitled to lose their cool once in a while. We are human and fallible and that's okay. I'm talking bout parents who abuse the use of discipline as a way to express their perpetual disapproval of their offspring. One of the saddest experiences to witness within a family therapy session is when the parents are just plain at fault, just plain wrong, and are totally responsible for the presenting problems. Yet, because of that wonderful hierarchical structure too many parents think that they are always right because they get to make the rules. And what if the rules that they make are simply disastrous and are likely the cause of the child's emotional difficulties? Let me give you an example.

I once saw a 16-year-old male patient who was riddled with anxiety. Upon first meeting him, I immediately felt a deep compassion and sympathy for him. He was the type of person who wore his anxiety from the top of his head to the bottom of his feet. Here is the parents' presentation of the problem: "He's being difficult. He refuses to remain in his sports club. It is 'mandatory' that he plays a sport. All of our children must do it. His grades are slipping. If he can get a 3.9

G.P.A., why can't he get a 4.0. Yes, we have strict expectations, but he must abide by them."

Now, what if the poor kid just wasn't interested in playing sports. It didn't matter to the parents. They weren't bending. After all, the father "had to" play sports when he was growing up so his children have to, as well. The underlying message from these parents to their children was that, "You need to be perfect and perform according to our standards in order for us to approve of you." Is it any wonder this poor kid was a nervous wreck? My heart felt for him because his parents weren't interested in the emotional well being of their son. The rules mattered more!

This leads to my next thought. When parents disapprove of their children's behavior, as a punishment they will often withdraw their love from them. Some parents explain this as a sort of self-imposed timeout. They may further justify their withdrawal with, "I'm too mad to even look at him and I don't trust what hurtful thing I might say." Well, the problem with this is that their child will interpret their reaction as, "Mom and dad don't love me," which makes them feel a sense of rejection and disapproval. Sure, if utilized in limited quantities, this type of dynamic may elicit positive behavior modification. However, if utilized in excess, the results could be quite detrimental to the sense of self-acceptance and self-approval of a developing child and adolescent. Remember the conversation about the continuum. Most behaviors and interactions are just a fine line away from being adaptive or maladaptive, or in some instances, appropriate or abusive.

You are probably getting the idea that I am very much an advocate for children. And, in fact, I am. However, I am also supportive of parents and enjoy working with them toward creating a healthier and more nurturing family environment. It is just that in all my years of counseling families, I have witnessed many parents hurting their children. I don't believe their behavior is intentional. It stems more from a lack of understanding about the dynamics of interpersonal relationships. Some parents often repeat the same mistakes that their parents made by simply behaving like their role models behaved with them.

The difficult aspect of family therapy is that the parents have to be open to looking at their own parenting skills as well as be willing to change and progress in a more positive direction. Some parents are concerned that if they change, then they are admitting that they are wrong. If parents admit that they are wrong, they fear that they will lose authority and credibility with their children. And, how can parents effectively manage their household and discipline their children if their authority and leadership is undermined and challenged? Well, these are valid concerns. However, I believe that positive adaptations to a family system are possible without disempowering the parental dyad. This is when therapy becomes more of an art than a science. A therapist needs to be a very skilled mediator in family therapy sessions.

I have treated a younger group of adolescents ranging from ages 12 through 15 with severe anxiety symptoms. Many of their stressors come from their parents' unrealistic perfectionistic expectations of them. Some of these parents were not able to fulfill their own life goals so they impose them onto their children regardless of whether it might be what the children want or need. Hence, my point about parents who regard their children as objects of possession. Many times parents will claim that, "All we want is what is best for our children." And, although there is likely some truth in this statement, often times what they really want is for their children to complete their unfinished goals, which, in fact, may not be in the best interest of their children.

I'm sure that you have heard that archaic expression from parents of a certain generation that children should, "Do as I say and not as I do." Yeah, right!! The truth of the matter is that there is a better likelihood that children will do more of what the parents do than what they say. Here is a good example. I was counseling a couple and the wife complained about how the husband withdraws from her when there is a problematic issue that they need to resolve. His typical behavior would be to "stomp up the stairs and slam the bedroom door." I asked them,

"Isn't that the exact behavior of your 13-year-old daughter that you were complaining about last week?"

Here's another example. A 14-year-old daughter is having "yelling and temper tantrum behaviors," and the parents did not understand why she was acting in this manner. It only took a couple of sessions to understand that "yelling" is the standard communication pattern of the parents and that their daughter was only emulating their behavior. Furthermore, because her parents were overly controlling, she felt that she could only be heard if she raised the volume of her voice. Parents who view their children as separate individuals will often give them a voice in matters, unlike parents who see their children as objects of possession without a voice of their own.

Parents who are overbearingly controlling of their children, especially during the developmental stage of adolescence wherein it is rather "normal" for teenagers to become more independent of their parents, will often complain that their children are "rebellious" and "out-of-control." The real difficulty with this type of dynamic is that the more controlling the parents try to be, the more the teenager will appear to rebel. Thus, it becomes a vicious cycle, with overly controlling parents unable to understand their contribution to the problem.

So what happens to adolescents who grow into adults still yearning for a sense of approval from their parents? Well, unfortunately there is a large group of the self-medicating type. I've treated many alcoholic and drug dependent and abusing adult patients over the years. Many of them are in denial that there is an underlying emotional issue behind their need to alter their reality with drugs or alcohol.

Lots of times I will ask a very direct question such as, "So why do you get high every night after work while your wife is preparing dinner for the family?" Or, "What is it that you like (I'm assuming that you like it since you do it every evening) about drinking until you've become intoxicated and incoherent?" I am always surprised when these patients look at me as if I'm speaking to them in a foreign tongue. Sometimes they think it's some sort of a trick question. I'll have to explain that I'm not trying to "trick" them. Rather, I'm trying to understand what they get from their chemical indulgences and altered realities. In other words, what is so wrong with your present reality that it needs to be altered? The sad truth about their inability to answer the question is that they have not thought much about it. Hence, my point about some of us being too busy living our lives without spending much time reflecting on our lives.

Other than not giving their addictive behavior patterns much thought because their life is too busy for self-reflection and introspection, many people are in denial of their addictions, which only come to the topic of a therapy session as a result of an ultimatum from their spouse/partner. Many of these patients with addiction problems were eventually able to unmask deep-seated emotional issues. Some drank to cover up their "social anxiety," cope with a poor self-esteem, alleviate their depressed moods, etc. Some patients are still searching for that ever-elusive parental approval.

To compensate for parental approval, some adults may become overachievers. The super dads, great husbands, dynamite employers/employees, etc., and this isn't necessarily a bad thing as long as you don't make yourself physically or psychologically ill along the way. This would be an adaptive way of trying to get your unmet emotional needs of earlier relationships met through current relationships. This is also another example of how many diverse experiences along life's journey can bring about emotional healing and fulfillment.

One of the reasons the issue of approval is difficult for patients to directly address in therapy is that it makes them feel quite vulnerable, and understandingly so. Most adults want to be self-assured and confident and have a sense of belief in themselves. So naturally it would be particularly unsettling to discuss the historical content, if not the current situations, that pertain to lacking a sense of approval and acceptance by the significant people in their lives.

I also realize that it is not common to speak in terms of "being approved of" and "accepted by" your loved ones. We don't speak using these terms directly because it makes us feel "too raw." But, I still believe that these needs are at the base of emotional fulfillment and a sense of self-acceptance. I may take a direct approach with sensitive issues because ironically, the more direct I am with patients, the more direct they can be in return and they don't waste time (as my mother would say) "beating around the bush." It's almost as if you can desensitize a patient (in a good way) by being very direct in that the issue is brought in the open and it's out there to be dealt with, and there is no need for embarrassment or shame. I'd like to think that my directness is tempered with a genuine empathy and compassion for my patients. Also, most patients seem to appreciate a direct approach.

Sometimes there is nothing more annoying for patients then when they ask a direct question, seeking a direct answer, only to have their therapist answer them with a question. Now, I'm sure there are times when that Counseling 101 approach would be appropriate. But I think that therapists need to be attuned to their patient's needs and answer the darn question if it's in the best interest of the patient. Therapists could always preface their reply with, "This is just my opinion but you are the one that must decide...." I think that it is important for therapists to be flexible and address their patient's needs. However, there are some theoretical orientations and styles of counseling that are not designed for flexibility within therapeutic interactions. It doesn't mean that these orientations and counseling styles are not effective forms of therapy. It means that patients need to find an appropriate therapeutic match with a therapist who they are comfortable with and can help facilitate their therapeutic goals.

A trusting and effective therapeutic alliance is especially important for patients seeking acceptance and approval since these needs may be met through the therapeutic relationship. Simply put, through transference, when the patient transfers feelings, thoughts, and emotional issues that they have toward others (e.g., their parents) onto the therapist (who my represent a parental figure), corrective emotional experiences could occur as a result of the therapist meeting unmet emotional needs.

This leads to our final "A"-that of Attention. Naturally, when people receive a sense of acceptance, affection, appreciation, and approval from other persons, they do so by people paying attention to them. So let's take a closer look at what it means to give attention to someone about whom we care.

Chapter V—Attention

The Random House Webster's College Dictionary defines attention as "the act or faculty of mentally concentrating on a single object, thought, or event, especially in preference to other stimuli; observant care or consideration; civility or courtesy; notice or awareness." The word "attentions" is defined as "acts of courtesy or devotion indicating affection." The adjective "attentive" is defined as "giving attention; observant; mindful; thoughtful of others; considerate; polite; courteous" (88). Wow, when you read this definition and apply it to the personal interactions between people who care about each other, giving and receiving attention sure sounds like great stuff!

So what are the ways that parents can give attention to their children? And, how do spouses/mates give attention to each other? According to the above definition, the approaches would appear to be endless. For example, we can pay attention to a loved one merely by being courteous and polite to him/her. We can pay attention simply be being a good listener. Just sit there and listen, blocking out all other distracting stimuli and focusing on the person with you. Another simple yet very attentive and intimate behavior that I enjoy in a personal relationship is when this special gentleman addresses me by my first name during the course of a conversation. It is warmly personal, and it makes me feel as if he is paying extra special attention to me.

Attention is another one of those emotional needs that a lot of us are not comfortable addressing directly. It may be hard for a mate to say to another, "Hey, I need some attention from you." Why is this so hard to say? Well, because it makes us feel vulnerable and feeling vulnerable often makes us feel needy. Many people worry that if they appear needy, they will appear "weak" and thereby lose their attractiveness to their mate. In addition, "feeling needy and weak" may also cause some people to feel less confident in themselves. So you see why speaking openly about your needs can be unnerving for some folks, especially for those who struggle with self-confidence issues. However, I think that it is important to understand that it is quite normal to have emotional needs, and that this is part of the essence of being human. An individual is not weak or needy for acknowledging his or her needs and in trying to have them fulfilled. There is no shame in needing others. But it is a shame if we sometimes let our pride distance us from being close and loving with others.

The problem with unmet attention needs that aren't adequately addressed and resolved is that they usually result in built-up anger, sadness, hurt, and resentment. And, what do you think happens to all those feelings? If you think that they may remain in a neat little compartment stored up for an explosive fit, you'd be right. Whenever I hear couples complain that they are quarrelling all the time about insignificant, petty issues, I often wonder if there may be deeper, more significant issues. For example, if one's attention needs aren't met, it is not uncommon that s/he will "flip out" over "nothing" as a way to vent the underlying hurt, anger, sadness, etc. about the more profound issues.

Now, don't get me wrong, sometimes being mad about the toilet seat being left up is just about the toilet seat. When the level or intensity of anger seems above and beyond what is justified for the offense, there may be a deeper issue that needs to be addressed. As I mentioned earlier, sometimes people aren't even aware of what is bothering them, which in turn makes it impossible to present to another so that it could be resolved. Attention to others requires an awareness of them. But, it is equally important to have an awareness of ourselves, especially if we are seeking emotional fulfillment.

Lacking awareness of others and not paying enough attention to them can sometimes result in taking them for granted. I don't think that this is intentional behavior meant to hurt another person. Rather,

I often think that it is more reflective of the fast-paced lives that we lead. It is almost as though we are too busy to be polite or courteous to others. This is one complaint that I often hear from couples. "She takes for granted all of the chores that I do around the house without showing any sense of gratitude." A simple "thank you" and "please" gives you an opportunity to be polite and courteous to your mate. But on a deeper level, you are letting your mate know that you are observant and mindful of him/her, that you are paying attention to all that they do, and that you are appreciative!

Some parents who are sterner in nature may think that they should not extend "pleases" or "thank yous" to their children when they do their "mandatory" tasks, e.g., cleaning their rooms, completing household chores, doing their homework, etc. Naturally, you don't have to say please and thank you every time a task is accomplished, but it wouldn't hurt to be courteous from time to time. You'd be setting a good example as well as providing verbal rewards for your child, who is more likely to repeat the behavior when positively reinforced for it. Furthermore, being gracious toward a child goes beyond being polite and courteous, it lets your child know that you are aware of him and his activities and that you are paying attention to him. A child whose attention needs are met is a child who is less likely to "act out" in order to get some attention from others.

I'm sure most of you have heard the expression in one form or another that, "Bad attention is better than no attention at all." And, is this ever true! Most adolescents that I've worked with who were "purposely" acting out were doing so as an attempt to get their parents to pay attention to them. Some adolescents would candidly admit that they were seeking attention while others would deny that their strategy was to garner a bit of attention from their parents. But, hey, there they are sitting in a therapy session with some direct, one-on-one attention from their parents, so look at all the attention that they are receiving.

At the risk of repeating myself, clothing, feeding, educating, and providing a roof for your children is only a small part of paying attention to them, but it shouldn't be the bulk of the attention that you dote on your children. The faster the pace of your professional life and the more demanding it is of your time, the more care you need to take in allotting quality time for your child. This is especially true if both parents work outside the home. Even with advanced technology and more parents working from home, this doesn't qualify as time with your child. I've worked with many parents who have conducted their business from a home office, and they confirmed that other than a couple of breaks to visit with family members, their primary focus was on work during hours designated for work.

I once treated a man whose wife had as demanding of a profession as he did. They both worked 10 to 12-hour days so they had a live-in nanny. Even when both he and his wife were home at night, their children would go to the nanny for anything that they needed, which hurt them very much. So remember, please, that attention is a two-way street, i.e., attention will likely be returned to the person who gives it, especially in regard to children and adolescents.

Why do you think that adolescents are so susceptible to peer influence? Sure, this is due in large part to that normal developmental stage wherein teens start to become independent of their parents and are more aligned with their peers. But, it is also a response to the very people who are giving them a lot of attention. So parents beware, you still need to spend quality time with your teens, especially if you want them to embrace and adopt your code of values and behaviors.

Listen, it may be a natural response to teens in this stage of their lives for parents to withdraw from them as a way of giving them space and freedom to become self-reliant. This is especially true when teens begin to drive and work a part-time job. However, not only is your guidance still needed but so is your love and affection. Too many teens become disconnected from their parents, and the results may not be positive. Often teens will sense this "disconnect" as a lack of attention and love from the parents, which in turn might lead to risky behaviors of drug/alcohol use, promiscuity, etc. So my advice to parents is to stay connected to your teenagers by giving them some good, old-fashioned attention.

Paying attention to those who rely on you for affection, appreciation, and approval is necessary in order to have all of these emotional needs met. It is not humanly possible to feel the joy of being accepted and appreciated by others if you feel ignored by them. How else would one receive affection and approval by another if not through some form of attention given to them?

You see, I think that the base of the 5 "As" is that of LOVE and ACTION, with love being the force behind the acts and expressions of acceptance, affection, appreciation, approval, and attention to others. So, you see, I prefer to think of love in terms of a verb. What good is love in the heart if it is not acted upon and expressed? Isn't love in the heart that is not expressed and not shared and not experienced between people a lost love?? And, love is too precious to lose by not acting upon it.

The journey to emotional fulfillment is an on-going, vital process, and we are active participants in this journey. All that is required is an awareness of our needs and wants and choices and the willingness to do our part to attain and maintain them. You see, once again, a rather simple concept, yet a profound one. But, I think that a life of depth is one worth living. And, a life worth living is surely one to be appreciated!!

References

Costello, Robert B., ed. <u>Random House Webster's College Dictionary</u>. 1987 ed.

978-0-595-48522-2
0-595-48522-7

Printed in Great Britain
by Amazon

MISCELLANEOUS

David Archard, **Meon Valley Printers**, Abbey Mill, Station Rd, Bishops Waltham, Hants, SO3 1DH. (Printer of all the NPF publications, and of this book).

Martin Taylor, **Imperial War Museum**, Lambeth Rd, London, SE1 6HZ. (Interested in obtaining complimentary copies of good war poetry for their collection).

Ivan Saunders, **Photographer**, 3 West Downs Close, Fareham, Hants. (First class colour or black and white photos of any subject processed suitably for book covers or illustration).

Tim Wiltshire, **Fine Bookbinder**, P G Wells Ltd, 11 College St, Winchester, Hants, SO23 9PZ. (For that one-off special copy bound in leather, and other specialist bindings).

The Forward Poetry Prizes, 9 Great Pulteney St, London, W1R 3DF. (Best collection £10,000, Best first collection £5,000, Best single published poem £1,000).

Wendy Goodman (**Advertising – The Writers News**), 94 Fore St, Heavitree, Exeter, Devon, EX1.

Eric Gregory Trust (Annual competitive award for poets under the age of 30) and **Cholmondeley Awards** (Annual non-competitive awards for poets) The Society of Authors, 84 Drayton Gdns, London, SW20 9SB.

Lynn Chambers, **Peterloo Poets Open Poetry Competition**, 2 Kelly Gdns, Calstock, Cornwall, PL18 9SA.

Stan Trevor, **Association of Little Presses**, 30 Greenhill, Hampstead High St, London, NW3 5UA. (A loose affiliation of small presses formed for their mutual benefit).

Arvon Foundation, Totleigh Bank, Heptonstall, Hebden Bridge, West Yorkshire, HX7 6DF. (Workshops and lectures).

Twiggers (out of print books). Tel: 0272 682155.

SELECTED POETRY PUBLISHERS

A
Peter Jay, **Anvil Press Poetry Ltd**, 69 King George St, London, SE10 8PX.

B
Anne Tannahill, **Blackstaff Press**, 3 Galway Park, Dundonald, Belfast, BT16 0AN
Neil Astley, **Bloodaxe Books Ltd**, PO Box ISN Newcastle Upon Tyne, NE99 1SN.

C
Kate Gavron, **Carcanet Press Ltd**, 208 Corn Exchange Buildings, Manchester, M4 3BQ.
Joy Hendry, **Chapman**, 4 Broughton Place, Edinburgh, EH1 3RX.

F
Faber & Faber, 3 Queen's Square, London, WC1N 3AU.

H
John Hale, **Robert Hale Ltd**, Clerkenwell House, Clerkenwell Green, London, EC1R 0HT.

L
Tony Ward, **Littlewood Arc**, Nanholme Mill, Shaw Wood Rd, Todmorden, Lancs, OL14 6DA.

N
Johnathon Clifford **The National Poetry Foundation** (Registered Charity No 283032) 27 Mill Rd, Fareham, Hants, PO16 0TH.

V
Leonore Goodings, **Virago Press Ltd**, Centro House, 20–23 Mandela St, London, NW1 0HQ.

Brian Merrikin Hill, **Pennine Platform**, Ingmanthorpe Hill Farm Cotage, Wetherby, W Yorkshire, LS22 5EQ.
Poetry & Audience, School of English, University of Leeds.
Poetry Durham, Michael O'Neill, Dept of English, Durham University, Elvet Riverside, New Elvet, Durham, DH1 3JT.
Poetry Nottingham, 21 Duncombe Close, Nottingham, NG3.
Tracey Walton, **Poetry Now**, 1-2 Wainman Rd, Woodstone, Peterborough PE2 7BU.
Peter Forbes, **The Poetry Review**, 22 Betterton St, London, WC2H 9BU.
Poetry Voice, 32 Ridgemere Rd, Pensby, Wirral, L61 8RL.
Poetry Wales, 26 Andrews Close, Heolgerrig, Mid Glam.
Geoff Stevens, **Purple Patch**, 8 Beaconview House, Charlemont Farm, W Bromwich, W Midlands, B71 3PL.

R
J Wakeman, **The Rialto**, 32 Grosvenor Rd, Norwich, NR2 .

S
Mark Robinson, **Scratch**, Cleveland Arts, 7-9 Eastbourne Rd, Linthorpe, Middlesborough, Cleveland, TS5 6QS.
Liz Reeve, **South**, 43 Avenue Rd, Wimborne, Dorset, BH21 1BS.
Donald Atkinson, **New Spokes**, The Orchard House, 45 Clophill Rd, Upper Gravenhurst, Bedford, MK45 4JH.

T
The Third Half, 16 Fane Close, Stamford, PE9 1HG.

W
Westwords, 15 Trelawney Rd, Peverell, Plymouth, PL3 4JS.
Weyfarers, 9 Whiterose Lane, Woking, Surrey, GU22 7JA.
The Wide Skirt, 93 Blackhouse Rd, Fartown, Huddersfield.
Writing Women, 10 Mistletoe Rd, Newcastle Upon Tyne.

Z
Z, 6a, Switzerland Terrace, Douglas, Isle of Man.

Judi Benson, **Foolscap**, 78 Friars Rd, East Ham, London,E6.
Jeremy Page, **The Frogmore Papers**, 131 North View Rd, Hornsey, London, N8 7RL.

G
Global Tapestry, 1 Springbank, Longsight Rd, Salebury, Blackburn, Lancs, BB1 9EU.
The Green Book, 49 Park St, Bristol, BS1 5NT.

H
Hat, 1A Church Lane, Croft, Nr Skegness, Lincs.

I
Lesi Markham, **Inkshed**, Flat 4, 387 Beverley Rd, Hull, HU5
David Holliday, **Iota**, 67 Hady Crescent, Chesterfield, Derbyshire, S11 0EB.
Peter Mortimer, **Iron**, 5 Marden Terrace, Cullercoats, North Shields, Tyne & Wear, NE30 4PD.

N
Network of Women Writers, 8 The Broadway, Woking, Surrey, GU21 5AP.
New Hope International, 20 Werneth Ave, Gee Cross, Hyle, Cheshire, SK14 5NL.

O
Mike Shields, **Orbis**, 199 The Long Shoot, Nuneaton, Warks, CV11 6JQ.
Eric Ratcliffe, **Ore**, 7 The Towers, Stevenage, Herts, SG1 1HE.
Richard Skinner, **Otter**, Parford Cottage, Chegford, Newton Abbot, Devon.
Roland John, **Outposts**, 22 Whitewell Rd, Frome, Somerset, BA11 4EL.

P
PAUSE, 27 Mill Rd, Fareham, Hants, PO16 0TH.
Pen umbra, 1 Beeches Close, Saffron Walden, Essex, CB11
Pennine Ink, The Gallery Downstairs, Yorke St, Burnley.

SELECTED POETRY MAGAZINES

A
Patricia Oxley, **Acumen**, 6 The Mount, Furzeham, Brixham, Devon, TQ5 8QY.
William Cookson, **Agenda**, 5 Cranbourne Court, Albert Bridge Rd, London, SW11 4PE.
Jean Barker, **Aireings**, 24 Broadenell Rd, Leeds, LS6 1BD.
Eddie Linden, **Aquarius**, Flat 3, 116 Sutherland Ave, London, W9.

B
John Osborne, **Bete Noir**, Dept of American Studies, Hull University, Cottingham Rd, Hull, HU6 7RX.
George Cairncross, **Bogg**, 31 Belle Vue St, Filey, Yorkshire, YO14 9HU.
Andrew Morrison, **Borderlines**, Anglo-Welsh Poetry, The Flat, Cronkhill, Crosshouse, Shrewsbury, SY5 6JP.
Dr Mario Petrucci, **The Bound Spiral**, 72 First Ave, Bush Hill Park, Enfield, EN1 1BW.
Clare Chapman, **Bradford Poetry Quarterly**, 9 Woodvale Rd, Bradford, BD7 2SJ.
Shetland Arts Trust, **Briggistane**, 22-24 North Rd, Lerwick, Shetland.

C
Cencrastus, 34 Queen St, Edinburgh, Scotland.
Joy Hendry, **Chapman**, 15 Nelson St, Edinburgh.
Dr Philip Higson, **Chester Poets**, 1 Westlands Ave, Newcastle, Staffs.
Peter Kenny, **Cobweb**, 7 Isis Court, Grove Park Rd, Chiswick London, W4 3SA.

E
Roger Elkin, **Envoi**, 44 Rudyard Rd, Biddulph Moor, ST8 7JN.

F
Josephine Austin, **First Time**, 4 Burdett Place, George St, Hastings, E Sussex TN34 3ED.

Arts Associations:
(Write to The Literary Officer).

Dr Alistair Niven (Literary Director), **The Arts Council of Great Britain**,14 Great Peter St,London, SW1P 3NQ.
Cleveland Arts, 7-9 Eastbourne Rd, Linthorpe, Middlesborough, Cleveland, TS5 6QS.
East Midlands Arts, Mountfields House, Forest Road, Loughborough, Leicestershire LE11 3HU.
Eastern Arts, Cherry Hinton Hall Cherry Hinton Rd Cambridge CB1 4DW.
Greater London Arts, Coriander Building, 20 Gainsford St, London SE1 2NE.
Merseyside Arts, Graphic House, Duke St, Liverpool L1 4JR.
North Wales Arts, 10 Wellfield House, Bangor, Gynedd LL57 1ER.
North West Arts, 12 Harter St, Manchester M1 6HY.
Northern Arts, 9-10 Osborne Terrace, Newcastle Upon Tyne NE2 1NZ.
South East Arts, 10 Mount Ephrain, Tunbridge Wells, Kent TN4 8AS.
South East Wales Arts, Victoria St, Cwmbran, Gwent, NP44 3YT.
South West Arts, Bradninch Place, Gandy St, Exeter, Devon, EX4 3LS.
Southern Arts, 19 Southgate St, Winchester, Hants, SO23 9DQ.
West Midlands Arts, 83 Granville St, Birmingham, B1 2LH.
West Wales Arts, Red St, Carmarthen, Dyfed, Wales SA31 1QL.
Yorkshire Arts, Glyde House, Glydegate, Bradford, W Yorkshire BD5 0BQ.
Scottish Arts, 24 Rutland Square, Edinburgh, Scotland, EH1 2BW

USEFUL ADDRESSES:

Recently I wrote to all the Central Libraries and asked them for a list of **poetry societies, clubs and groups** in their areas. As a result I have compiled a list that, if printed here, would take up another book. However, if you want information about a particular group or groups within a given area you may ring us on 0329 822218 (office hours *only* please) and we may be able to help, or, if not, put you onto someone who can.

Grants are always very difficult to find – start by reading the *Directory of Grant Making Trusts* in your local Reference Library or write direct to its publisher: **The Charities Aid Foundation**, at 48 Pembury Rd, Tonbridge, Kent, TN9 2JD.

What can only be described as the most comprehensive and informative of all the writing magazines is *The Writers News and Writing* (which has monthly poetry workshops by Alison Chisholm and Doris Corti). Edited by Richard Bell, available from: **Writers News Ltd**, P O Box 4, Nairn IV12 4HU.

How To Write For Publication by Chriss McCallum (now going into its 3rd edition): How To Books Ltd, Plymbridge House, Estover Rd, Plymouth PL6 7PZ.

The Author is the organ of The Society of Authors and available from: **The Society of Authors**, 84 Drayton Gdns, London, SW10 9SB.

Specialist information may be obtained from: **The Book Trust**, 45 East Hill, Wandsworth, London SW18 2QZ.

Ah! that I could be a fly on the wall of some college or university in the year AD 2193. What then will be the poetry read, loved and admired?

That which the Establishment would lead us to believe will be the case . . ?

Who knows! That will be their epitaph and . . .
    this book's.

ever became so, or even tried to be, then the whole mood and tenor of the poetry world would change overnight.

If, when members of the general public rang for information, they were met with a helpful, friendly and informative response, instead of a disembodied voice that appears to be trying to hide something, or give away as little as possible, perhaps the general public impression of the PS would be improved – I've tried ringing on occasions with simple, straightforward questions, only to be met with supercilious comments from very self-important sounding people (who had no idea of who I was) who gave the impression that all was far too much trouble!

It is also a well documented fact that if someone has come to rely on a 'freebie' for a long period there is little effort made to be in any way independent – perhaps it would be a good thing if the PS was to lose its grant and have to look for ways to self-finance. There are some aspects of the Poetry Society's activities which *should* be self-financing – poetry readings being a prime example of an area that could be made to make profits for the Society, with no doubt many others if a proper in-depth study was undertaken.

If the PS doesn't change, sooner or later – Arts Council's protective custody not withstanding – the genuine needs of poets and poetry will metaphorically pull it apart.

Perhaps, of the heirarchy that has controlled Poetry and the services offered to poetry for so long, it should be said:

"the mental stature warrants not the extra size."

changes at the Poetry Society (one of the long line of apparently powerless Literary Directors at the Arts Council) has tackled the initial problem, followed then by the entire membership of the Society throwing out the lees, the dregs, the chaff and the drones, *nothing* will ever change and the Society will never throw off its reputation as ineffectual and petty and become *the* authoritative, knowledgable and helpful senior poetry organisation in the UK which, once it has honestly earned it, **is its proper place.**

There would also seem to be some sense in *The Poetry Review*, edited by Peter Forbes (a solid editor who should be, and *be seen to be*, free of any restraint), being set up and funded as a separate entity so that it can be totally above any 'closed-shop loyalties'. Clive Wilmer in *The Times Saturday Review* of February 27th 1993 calls it "the official magazine of the Poetry Society."

That such a magazine should be referred to, almost automatically, as "The Poetry Society's official magazine," when it *should be* referred to as the National Poetry Magazine (totally independent of and from *anyone*), shows a part of the malaise in broad daylight. In 1988 when I asked that *The Poetry Review* advertise a charity poetry competition for me I was told that it was "too near their own competition for them to advertise." (This, in spite of the fact that it would have cost the NPF some £174 for them to do so. They were turning down income).

The Society's Charter must then be made openly more democratic and the PS clearly run within the rules of both a Public Society and Registered Charity.

But, apart from the Poetry Society becoming more Nationally accountable, every poetry society, group, club and individual throughout the UK, should feel able to look to the Society for advice, help, information and support.

This is supposed to be THE National poetry body, if it

been deeply dissatisfied with its organisation.

5) Why the one person who can flush out and freshen the Society, namely the Literary Director at the Arts Council, has, through the decades, never done so and always appeared extremely coy and evasive when tackled about what is being done.

My only personal comment has to be: with all that public money involved it's high time the Poetry Society became much more open in its dealings and all its Officers aware that they are supposed to be <u>Servants To Poetry</u> and not, Servants Of The PS – think about it! And that someone must be put in to administer it *properly*; having real authority to say 'what shall be done' – this, only after a secret postal election of *all* its officers by an independent pollster used to handling large postal ballots.

In virtually any instance 'What' depends exclusively on 'how' and 'by whom'. One of our subscribers tells me that before she joined the NPF she rang the Poetry Society to ask their advice on the best magazines to which she might subscribe. I quote her reporting of the conversation verbatim:

She:	Can you give me a list of the better magazines?
PS:	Are you politically active?
She:	No.
PS:	Are you a member of an ethnic group?
She:	No.
PS:	Are you a lesbian?
She:	No.
PS:	Well I'm afraid I can' t help you.

(this, to a highly respectable middle-aged lady). An example of 'what', the 'by whom' and the 'how'.

Until the only person who can insist on rigorous basic

Alastair Niven of the Arts Council was also present at this meeting – who informs me in his letter of 30th July 1993 that "The Arts Council does not appoint the Director of the Poetry Society, though we do have an observer status . . ." A month later, Sebastian Barker wandered into Paul Ralph's office and handed him a written "resign or be fired" ultimatum. Perhaps they 'only sack who do not hire'n fire'!?

As I say, I could not have found a man more 'behind' the Poetry Society, more attuned to trying to make it more efficient, more user-friendly. Yet he was accused of being responsible for its lack of identity, sense of purpose, and of not having the financial gumption to run it. Now Chris Green (Paul Ralph's replacement) is also to leave – of what, I wonder, does *he* stand accused?

News Flash – another unsuitable head rolls at the PS?

Meanwhile it will be interesting to note that Paul Ralph has set up and manages a company with an annual turnover of £0.5 million, while Sebastian Barker busies himself with . . . he and Fleur Adcock, choosing *Best Young Poets of the Year* . . . between them.

Perhaps Paul should still be with the Poetry Society? Sebastian elsewhere?

I pass on these facts simply so that you, reader, may make your own judgement and perhaps also ask the questions:

1) Why the Poetry Society has allegedly always been so strangely and poorly run.

2) How a Public Society can be organised so secretively.

3) Why so many of its Officers resign.

4) Why so many poets have for decades apparently

should be aware of the nature of these "stringent targets" demanded so that all interested parties may judge that they have genuinely been carried out within the time-period stipulated.

One problem the Society has always had is that there is no-one (as far as can be seen) who actually runs it. No-one who has ultimate control and a visible and ultimate responsibility – the Secretary/Director has a grand title, but it seems marginally next best to meaningless when it comes to clout!

The previous incumbent (Paul Ralph), came down for a beans-and-bacon lunch and a chat in 1988. He wanted to see if there were any points of contact possible between our two organisations and what we, at the Foundation, got up to.

He could not have been more stoutly enthusiastic about the work of the Poetry Society, nor would he hear a single word said against it. He felt (where the Poetry Society resources were concerned) two of the most important elements were, that their charter should be radically overhauled and democratised and that the white-elephant of a building in which they were housed should be sold – I gather he had in fact received a firm offer of some £200,000 in excess of the figure obtained when the building was eventually sold some time later. I also understand from him that as a reward for his efforts, Sebastian Barker (Chairman of the Society) called a meeting on 22nd February 1989 at which he presented a paper called *A Sense of Direction*, and proceeded to blame the luckless Paul Ralph for the lack of enthusiasm and direction at the Poetry Society (at the time Paul had been in office for eighteen months. Eighteen months in which he was to have cleared the eighty-year heap of steaming effluent from the Poetic stables?

News Flash – Hercules Ralph found wanting indeed!).

to a letter I received from Dr Alastair's predecessor in 1981 – nothing! The fact that (and I know the Poetry Society is a society though I did not until now realise that it was a masonic, magic or a secret one!) everything is, as always, "confidential." Not to be divulged.*WHY?!*

You can draw one parallel between the NPF and the Poetry Society and that is that we are both registered charities.

I understand from the Charity Commissioners that later this year (1993) it is to become law that if anyone wishes to know what any charity's money is spent on and what it gets up to, they can (for a fair small fee) have a copy of that charity's annual financial report to the Commissioners.

Why is it a case (and it has been forever-and-a-day) that what goes on at the Poetry Society is such a secret? Are they not using public funds (what else is a grant but tax payers' money?). Hasn't that tax payer the right to know what is going on behind the façade of what is supposed to be a public society – of course he has!

So let's see this nonsensical secrecy done away with once and for all, for it has gone on for far too long, and has, it is presumed, kept the Society's own members in the dark in so much as they do not know (for instance) what "stringent targets" their own Society has been set. The members should have been circulated such information by their executive committee as a matter of course as soon as the ultimatum had been made. At the end of these 'numbered months during which such earth-moving changes are to be made', who (when the grant is automatically renewed as it always has been and will forever be, Amen) will be the arbiter? Who say that the changes have been satisfactorily completed? Who judge? Perhaps the Poetry Society? The Arts Council? Never the members! Never the public whose money is used (or perhaps misused?).

This concerns a huge amount of public money. *Everyone*

Now, once again in this oft-in-each-decade token operation, it's happening. The Arts Council has threatened to withhold or withdraw its grant to the Poetry Society unless . . . hang on. Let me quote Dr Alastair Niven, (Literature Director at the Arts Council), in his letter to me dated July 21st '93:

Dear Mr Clifford,

Thank you for your letter of the 14 July 1993 concerning The Poetry Society. As always your comments are interesting and at times close to the point! The Poetry Society has recently been appraised and although at the moment the contents of the report are confidential we have already issued a press release indicating that the Arts Council's grant to the Society will be withdrawn in October 1994 if certain stringent targets are not met. Chris Green, the current director of the Society, has already indicated his intention to leave and it will be during the period in which these targets have to be achieved that a new director will be taking up the post. I hope that he or she will see the targets as a challenge rather than a millstone. I think everyone involved with the Society's affairs here will concur with your view that the person administering the Poetry Society should love poetry, be able to handle finance, and be without a dominating ego! I am also attracted to your idea of a reducing grant to the Society, which is really the model which many Arts Council clients should be adopting.

Thank you again for writing.

With best wishes,

Yours sincerely

Dr Alastair Niven
Literature Director

A polite and friendly letter giving the impression that as the Poetry Society is being run somewhat unsatisfactorily, things are most definitely being done. The big fist shaken, etc. So what's wrong with the letter, you ask.

Apart from the fact that it bears a startling resemblance

facility (it is far easier to run a pc than one of the old fashioned printing presses!) to set up a magazine or to publish a book. It has also led to an amazing amount of prose, weak verse and frankly, pure rubbish, being published by some small presses in the name of poetry, but this *doesn't matter*. The important thing is that work is *being* published. That which is of value poetically is far more likely to find its mark, than it was when it relied on the Establishment to notice its quality – unless it emanated directly from Oxbridge.

It is against this background and the Establishment's apparent ability to be blinkered and twenty years behind the times, that we have to look at organisations such as

THE POETRY SOCIETY: There have been many reasons given every time (during the last 30 years) that a threat has been made by the Arts Council to withhold the Poetry Society's grant:

"The *Poetry Review* was full of poetry containing 'rude words'.

Funds were being used 'unwisely'.

'They' cannot run within their budget but are always in the red.

'They' do sweet f.a. for poetry other than in London and the Home Counties."

All very solid reasons for a radical shake-up of the Poetry Society heirarchy – which of course (apart from minor cosmetics) has never happened – Why? Because the real problems have been studiously ignored by one Literary Director at the Arts Council after another.

CHAPTER XI

ART INSANITY: The advent of frames filled with dirty nappies; chimpanzees daubing at canvasses; bricks arranged in the same manner that Fred, on his morning shift at the brickyard, does it – all exhibited as Art of the highest calibre – composers filling their bars with notes that, far from being members of the same family, seemed not even on nodding let alone speaking terms – lauded as fine Music – and other such phenomena, showed that society in general and the Establishment in particular was undergoing some slight crisis of identity.

A similar situation existed in poetry – "See if you can get more Greek or Latin references in your poem than anyone else, or, spread the words all over the page so that they cannot possible do anything but bamboozle a reader, and we'll tell everyone what a fine poet you are!"

Mr Average in the street took one look at all this and decided it was not for him . . .

What reminds us of our childhood is to be cherished and looked back upon with longing and a belief that things were "better then." It is little wonder that Mr Average was convinced that the poetry written was only for the limp-wristed effete intellectual and not for *him* in any way at all. Was in fact simply meaningless, senseless and tasteless, while the poetry of his school-days was what he remembered as *good* poetry. . .

He was wrong, for of course there was good meaningful poetry being written, it was just that not much seemed to get to the public, thanks to or via the Establishment.

During the last thirty or forty years a sense of sanity has slowly returned. This process has been very much enhanced and speeded up with the advent of desk top publishing, for it became possible both from the point of finance and

Dear Johnathon,
    Just a note to thank you for your letter and to send my warmest congratulations to you on the establishment of the Foundation. A tremendous achievement. All power to your elbow.

Ted (Lord Willis) 25. 6. 81

    I could go on and on with these snippets from letters; some pleasant, others bitchy and bad tempered – all those reproduced here are done so with a smile (on my part), whether they be complimentary or otherwise.

    I'm not sure that I haven't included more 'miserable' ones than those 'in praise of', there <u>are</u> certainly many more that are in praise of, than those that are not.

    Perhaps it is a question that I value the 'grubby' ones as much if not more than those in praise – it helps keep one's feet firmly on the floor to remind oneself that one is not considered brilliantly-helpful and wonderful and good and nice and noble by . . .

quite everyone!

. . . before submitting more poems I'd like to make a few comments, although it is quite likely that having read those comments you will not be requiring futher submissions.
C P 1. 6. 92.

Dear Johnathon,
Thank you for the parcel of books and information you sent to me so quickly after our recent telephone conversation. I hadn't realised how much the Poetry Foundation did for authors.
Broadcast Books 25. 1. 93

Dear Mr Clifford,
Such a pity that the NPF is to me such a disappointment. It sounded so good in theory. But then; so is politics and religion. Theory and practice so seldom equate.
Frank B B 18. 11. 92

Dear Johnathon,
Mea Culpa! It appears that I never wrote that cheque to order more books. I've checked with the bank and it has never gone through my account.
Sheila G B 23. 11. 92

Dear Mr Clifford,
. . . the children were both surprised and thrilled with your decisions and we managed to put up a display of all the poems at Speech-day
Lesley D (teacher) 9. 6. 92

(Author's note: Our standard intro letter stresses that . . . poetry must be typed)

Dear Johnathon,
I thank you for your leaflet, about your new book. Seeing as you, keep so rigid (sic), *to your rules, I shall decline, the offer. I make my own rules, as far as any of my work is concerned.* (I'd written asking her to have her poems typed) *I don't even own, a typewriter, I presumed, that was the editors work. If you, cannot have the courtesy, to read, my work, why on earth, should I, take the time, and trouble, to read yours.*
signed by Margaret
M J 15.10.93

(All this in the most illegible script)

Dear Sirs,
    Please would you be good enough to forward me an application form for some financial assistance, since being off nursing eighteen months ago I have been trying to become self-sufficent as a poet, but I am unable to progress.
A S-B 16. 9. 93

Dear Madam,
    Thankyou for the return of my unsuccessful entries for the PHRAS93 OPEN POETRY COMPETITION. The enclosures relating to your strategy for chosing the winning entries impressed me as being thoughtful, realistic and fair. I was delighted to receive your brief synopsis and comments on the winning entries.
L W 15. 6. 93

. . . my poems (4 were submitted for the Phras93) were returned. Poets and writers get rejection slips all the time. But I wonder if any before have been forced to read such a callous, self-righteous explanation? I've never heard or read a more insulting commentary.
N M B 19. 6. 93

Dear Miss,
    Sorry I forgot to enclose a stamp – I must thank you for the very useful document on how the competition was judged. That kind of feedback is invaluable for preparation for future entries.
John T 29. 6. 93

Dear Organiser,
    Obviously no-one read my poetry or I would have won a prize.
J. J 24. 6. 93

(Author's note: this was the start of a three page abusive letter – you wouldn't believe the four letters above were written about the same competition)

Dear Johnathon and Helen,
    I have a fair number of words at my disposal (usually) but can only be silent in the matter of your commitment on my behalf . . . Such effort deserves rather more than an insipid 'thank you'.
Bill L 3. 5. 93

Dear Johnathon,
 Please find four poems enclosed. I have been writing poems from my childhood because when I am old and grey, about childhood memories – about things I did not want to forget. (sic) Thank you for your comments on the last poem especially 'invisible boy' I retyped it as you suggested and I am happy to leave it out.
Joy A 8. 2. 87

Dear Johnathon,
 I am returning the poem, but I have changed the name, also the first ~~andsl~~ (sic) of the first verse and the last. It now sounds to me, somewhat improved, what on earth would I do without you! I do not know, and more important, what would poetry do!
M 4. 7. 88

Dear Mr Clifford,
 Thank you for your letter dated 24 March and earlier communications. Unfortunately I can see no point in pursuing this any further . . . Obviously you simply do not like my poems. I can understand this – there are many poets and would-be poets whose work I do not appreciate myself.
B M C 20. 3. 92

Dear JC,
 That was quite a day! Speaking to you on the phone and hearing you on radio (even if I had to listen through "fur coat and no knickers" first!). I have always thought of you as a man of feeling – especially in your damning castigations! Now I can tell you have a splendid speaking voice and come across full of vitality. If you need anything retyped just let me know.
Hope R 1. 9. 88

Dear Johnathon,
 I was sorry to hear about your eye and I hope things have improved post operatively. I have read your letter of the 14th several times and you have made a great deal of sense . . . I shall constantly refer to this letter.
Rod W 20. 8. 89

Dear Johnathon,
 I do not wish to receive any more leters (sic) which are an insult to my intelligence and education.
Sandra G 14. 3. 92

Dear John,
 . . . I'll distribute your book ~~secretly~~ selectively, I hate the thought of anything small press being picked up and put in the bin.
Tom B 29. 1. 87

Dear Johnathon,
The trouble is that there are about 600 poems, some good, some needing work, which he had been keeping in a suitcase until I found out about them . . . we work happily if slowly . . . we are also tearing up the bad ones.
Celia R 27. 1. 87

Dear Mr Clifford
It is really very good to see someone doing something towards helping poets get published.
P.F.G 18. 4. 84

Dear Johnathon,
I couldn't believe my eyes when I opened your letter this morning and read that you'd accepted one of my poems.
Maire E 5. 2. 88

Dear Sir,
Many, many thanks for the briliant critique that accompanied the poems you returned to me. It's the best I've had. What a marvellous service to the poet.
John B 3. 12. 86

Dear Mr Clifford,
I am returning your begging letter which has just been forwarded from my previous address. I stated in my last letter that I did not want to receive anymore correspondence from either you or your 'foundation' any further communication from you will be forwarded unread to my waste paper basket. I regret I am unable to subscribe to 'Some Vast And Hideous Army' because I can only assume that your poetry has no more substance than your criticism.
A B 20. 2. 88

Dear Sir/Madam,
I am applying to your Foundation for a grant so I can be an aspiring poet, it is very expensive being out of work.
S V 14. 7. 93

CHAPTER X

One of the outstanding joys of running any sort of mail orientated organisation is of course the mail. Over the years I have received literally thousands of letters from subscribers, from members of the general public and from some prize idiots.

LETTERS: A long time ago I decided that I would keep a file of all the ego-boosting letters so that, in low moments, I could read them. Interspersed with them I included all the angry, insane, furious letters – the one as a mental balance, as it were, against the other. One could, with such a file to hand, never become too despondent nor too over-bearingly self-satisfied!
I thought you might enjoy a few of them:

Dear Mr Clifford,
Thank you for your last letter and my immediate thought was 'What's the man talking about' but by the time I read it again I knew you were on the right track and that's the type of criticism we need
Dave S 6. 9. 87

Dear John,
Thank you so much for the anthology which has failed to arrive.
Pat L 18. 10. 87

Dear Johnathon,
I have been meaning to send you this for months . . . I do heartily agree with your rule that no-one connected with the Foundation can benefit from it.
Margaret T 14.12.87

Dear Sir,
I'm in prison because I stole a large amount of money from the post office to come to England to see my parents, but I'm in prison so didn't come.
L.G (Ireland) 17. 4. 87

Perhaps one of the problems is that in the choosing of the Poet Laureate there seems to be not the slightest consideration for whether the person likely to be chosen has any ability whatsoever to fill the situation vacant, and that, having been chosen, he is simply left out in the cold at the mercy of Joe Public who often (and with some good reason) decides the incumbent of the position is "pretty much useless as a poet and not much good on telly either!" Something that of course not only doesn't help the image of the position of Poet Laureate, but also does very little for poetry itself along the way.

properly and easily). Learn the poems you are to recite so that your concentration is on the expression, not on remembering the words (but do have a copy of what you are to read with you, or you'll likely dry-up).

Some of these problems are to be found even amongst those who've reached that highest accolade attributed to any poet, that of being made

THE POET LAUREATE - a post few, if any, are prepared for in any way at all.

Personally I feel there should be a baby laureate's school! Here, from an early age would be trained a group of possibles (rather in an eastern sort of way) for the eventuality that each or any one of them might be chosen as the reincarnation of the last PL!

How to (publically) read his work; how to be at ease in company; how to write a poem at the drop of a hat on such riveting subjects as . . . The (yet-another) Royal Baby . . . Her or His Majesty's Birthday/Coronation/Anniversary/ Death/Marriage or whatever is apposite for the moment; how to be courteous rather than a boor (yes, and a bore as well!).

The problem is that there is some poor ol' poet, minding his own, as it were, trotting out his occasional ode with not a care in the world and suddenly - he's Poet Laureate! It might well be a great honour, but it is one that few are able to handle.

It is of course monstrous to expect anyone to compose a poem on any subject almost at the drop of a hat and then parade him and it around all the national media, for both to be dissected and either approved or, more normally, pulled apart and dismissed. Remember the adage that it is *not so much what you write, but what you choose to submit for publication* that is important? What chance our poor PL there!

CHAPTER IX

At this stage you've most of what you need to write poetry, apart from the other ingredient –

ABILITY: Poetry as an art form is very akin to painting or playing the piano. You can be taught scales and arpeggios until they come out of your ears, but if you don't practise you'll never make the grade.

You can be taught how to use pencils, pen, crayon, conté, brushes, paints; the art of perspective and how to look, and see what you're looking at. But if you don't practise you'll never make a painter.

It's the same with poetry. You can pick up techniques for expressing yourself, of being able to say *what* you want *how* you want, but if you don't practise your poetic art you won't pass muster as a poet.

One thing of course that all three have in common – you can be taught the basics, but you cannot be taught to be brilliant – that, whether as a pianist, painter or poet, has to be in you from the beginning.

Something else that few people seem to bother to learn (and it can and should be learnt) is how to recite poetry.

Let us start with the premis that extremely few poets are able to recite their own poetry (well anyway, without training) because they are much too 'close' to it. By 'close' I mean that when a poet recites one of his own poems he thinks he's expressing the emotional content of what he wrote, but because he knows the poem so well it all stays in his own mind, the reading being an invariable boring monotone. It is important to try and learn how to make somewhat less of a pig's left hind leg of it, so when reading your poetry aloud to an audience . . . stand, (don't sit or slouch, it compresses your diaphragm so you can't breathe

Punctuation. When writing poetry remember you are not writing prose! What you are trying to say does not rely on what, in prose, would be the perfect way to punctuate a sentence. You are writing music rather than prose when you write poetry so if, for argument's sake you want to say:

> great grey pounding powerful waves destroyed...

don't spoil it by saying:

> great, grey, pounding, powerful, waves destroyed...

The commas ruin the smooth flow of what you are saying and waves do not stop-start, stop-start, stop-start, (which is what all those commas make your eye do) waves run in smoothly all in one motion. By the same token don't fall into the trap (as so many seem to) of "if I'm not sure stick in a comma, semicolon, colon, full stop − anything rather than virgin fresh air − at the end of every line." This is called
End Stopping, and can completely shatter any smooth flow there might have been to the reading of your poem. Remember that the eyes' jump from the end of one line to the beginning of the next *creates a comma's worth of space anyway*.

Identical Rhyme. Occurs when the same word is used twice - considered to be a fault unless done deliberately for emphasis
Example:

> "He gave his bridle reins a shake,
>   Said "Adieu for evermore,
>   My love!
>   And adieu for evermore."
>
> Scott

Light Rhyme. Occurs when a stressed word is rhymed with the final unstressed syllable of the other word in a rhyming pair.
Example:

> "She looked over his shoulder
>   For vines and olive trees,
> Marble well-governed cities
>   And ships upon untamed seas."
>
> Auden

Alliteration. The repetition of initial consonants in a line of verse or closely adjacent lines. A kind of reversed rhyme, also known as 'initial rhyme', or 'head rhyme'.
Example:

> "Full fathom five thy father lies."
>
> Shakespeare

* * *

So now, hopefully, you are armed with some of the pebbles you'll need for your poetic slingshot to which I shall throw in just one more:

Apocopated Rhyme. Rhyme in which the end of one word is cut off.
Example:

"He with his famous history of New **Spain**
This priest is a learned man: is not ignorant:
And I am poor: without gold: **gain**less."
                                            MacLeish

OTHER RHYME FORMS:

Eye Rhyme. Occurs when words rhyme only to the eye.
Example:

   love/move,   strive/live

Historical Rhyme. Occurs when words that were pronounced alike in the past are now pronounced differently.
Example:

   wind/mind   (*wind used to be pronounced wynd*)

Cockney Rhyme. Occurs when two words which do not rhyme perfectly in Standard English are used by a poet who pronounces one or both of them with a Southern accent.
Example:

   faces/vases,   briar/attire

Rime Riche. Occurs when the rhyming words are identical in sound although the sense differs.
Example:

"And sikerly she was of great des<u>port</u>
And full pleasant, and amiable of <u>port</u>"
                                            Chaucer

When consonant sounds either side of the vowel are the same, it is known as Consonantal Dissonance.
Example:

> "Sit on the bed. I'm blind and three parts shell.
> Be careful, can't shake hands now: never shall.
> Both arms have mutinied against me – brutes,
> My fingers fidget like ten idle brats."
>
> Owen

Analysed Rhyme. A clever combination of assonance and consonance which has to be analysed to be appreciated. In a 4 line stanza, the consonants of the end rhymes in the 1st and 4th lines are the same, as are those of the 2nd and 3rd lines; while the vowels of the end rhymes of the 1st and 3rd lines match; as do those of the 2nd and 4th.
Example:

> "That night when joy began
> Our narrowest veins to flush,
> We waited for the flash
> Of morning's levelled gun."
>
> Auden

Amphisbaenic or **Backward Rhyme.** A clever combination of consonant assonance and dissonance, in which the consonants are reversed and the vowels remain the same.
Example:

> "But tonight I come alone and <u>belated</u> –
> Foreseeing in every <u>detail</u>
> And resolved for a day to side<u>step</u>
> My friends and their guests and their <u>pets</u>."
>
> Wilson

Vowel Rhyme. Any vowel is allowed to rhyme with any other.
Example:

"Of Tassels – and of Coaches – soon –
It's easy as a Sign –
The intuition of the News –
In just a Country Town –"
                                              Emily Dickinson

Assonance. (Also known as vocalic assonance). Occurs when the stressed vowels in the words are the same, but the consonants are not.
Example:

"Now as I was young and easy under the apple boughs
About the lilting house and happy as the grass was green,
The night above the dingle starry,
    Time let me hail and climb
Golden in the heydays of his eyes,
And honoured among wagons I was prince of the apple towns,
And once below a time I lordly had the trees and leaves
    Trail with daisies and barley
Down the rivers of the windfall light,"
                                              Thomas

Consonance. (Also known as Consonantal). Occurs when final consonants are the same but the vowels differ.
Example:

"Move him into the sun,
Gently its touch awoke him once,
At home, whispering of the fields unsown.
Always it awoke him, even in France,
Until this morning, and this snow."
                                              Owen

Triple, Tumbling or Three-syllabled Rhyme. Rhyme in which a stressed syllable is followed by two unstressed. Example:

> "Stranger! Approach this spot with gravity:
> John Brown is filling his last cavity."
>
> Anon

Broken Rhyme. A rhyme made up of more than one word. Example:

> "I went in vain to look for <u>Europolis,</u>
> Down in the Strand, just where the <u>new pole is</u>;
> For I can tell you one thing, **that I can**,
> You will not find it in the **Vatican**."
>
> Swift

Complete Rhymes. Also known as 'full',or 'perfect' rhymes, are exact rhymes where the words rhyme perfectly with each other. They have:

a) Identically pronounced vowel sounds.
b) Identically pronounced consonants following the vowels, if any.
c) Difference in the consonant sounds that precede the vowel.
d) Identical stressing of the two rhyming words or parts of words.

<u>POETICAL LICENCE IN THE USE OF RHYME</u>:

Near Rhyme. Also known as 'half rhyme', 'off rhyme', 'appropriate rhyme', 'oblique rhyme', 'imperfect rhyme', 'paraphones' or 'pararhymes'. In this type of rhyme similar rather than identical sounds are used.

Interlaced or Crossed Rhyme. This breaks a long rhyming couplet into four short lines with alternating rhymes.
Example:

"Will ye bridle the deep sea with <u>reins</u>, will ye chasten
      the high sea with **rods**?
Will ye take her to chain her with <u>chains</u>, who is older
      than all ye **Gods**?"
                                        Swinburne

Linked Rhyme. A rhyme made by linking the final syllable of one line with the first sound of the following line.
Example:

"Dame at our **door**
Drowned, and among our shoals,
Remember us in the roads the heaven-haven of the **reward**:
Our king back, Oh, upon English souls!"
                                        Hopkins

Random Rhyme. Rhyme which seems to occur accidently in any combination of the foregoing, often mixed with unrhymed lines.

CLASSIFICATION OF RHYMES BY SYLLABLES:

Masculine, Male or Single Rhyme. Rhyme in which the final syllable is stressed.
Example:
        cage/rage,   support/resort

Feminine, Female, or Double Rhyme. Rhyme in which the syllable before last is stressed.
Example:
        revival/arrival,   duty/beauty

I have simply said which words here take an emphasis in the reader's subconscious mind, I haven't gone into which words take the heavier or lesser stress, but this to some degree is governed by whether that word comes at the end or the beginning of a line and the basic meaning of what is being said anyway.

The use of rhyme itself and where it comes in a line (it doesn't, as some would have you believe, have to only come at the end of lines) can affect, create or muffle emphasis, as I'm sure you will appreciate from the pages which follow.

CLASSIFICATION OF RHYMES BY PLACE IN POEM:

End Rhyme. That which occurs at the end of lines.

Internal Rhyme. That which occurs within the lines.
Example:

"All is reaped now; no grass is left to **mow**;
And we that **sow**ed, though all we fell on sleep,
She would not weep."
Swinburne

Also called **Leonine Rhyme** when the first half of the line rhymes with the second, the internal rhyme occurring at the medial pause of the line, thus breaking the longer line into two short ones.
Example:

"The ice did split, with a thunder-fit . . ."
Coleridge

Oh deep blue water where
the Kutkuiece have fished,
impart your peace, to this
my troubled mind –
bequeath
your sure tranquility.

Oh deep blue water where the Kutkuiece have fished,
impart your peace to this, my troubled mind – bequeath
your sure tranquility.

Oh deep blue water
where the Kutkuiece have fished,
impart your peace to this my troubled mind,
bequeath your sure tranquility.

By stopping the end of the lines, or running them on, a slightly different emphasis is created. Let us try a more simplistic sentence to make the idea perhaps more easily understood: "I will not go out after dark," can have its emphasis radically altered by the way in which you lay it out:

>I will not
>go out after
>dark

(emphasis on the 'not', 'go', 'after' and 'dark')

>I will
>not go out
>after dark

(emphasis on 'will', 'not', 'out', 'after' and 'dark')

>I
>will not go out
>after dark

(emphasis on 'I', 'will', 'not' 'after' and 'dark')

use of archaic words or phraseology, or inverted and weak rhyme. It is no longer acceptable to use such words as 'tis, 'twas, e'er and o'er, and words such as hark, comely, yea, sere and knell are old-fashioned. In other words your poetry should be expressed in words and phrases in common usage. In the example of tetrameter I quoted a Collins poem, the first line being an inversion simply to get a rhyme with 'sung' – the more acceptable modern way of expresing this would be:

"Their knell is rung by fairy hands."

and were you to offer an inverted line as weak as that original to an editor today, it would certainly not be accepted.

A weak rhyme is where it is blatantly obvious that a word has been thought of which will rhyme and then a sentence contrived around getting that word at the end of the line with little or no thought of the sense of the sentence. The rhyme is all – sap the sense!

There is no magical language in which to write poetry, only the poetic use of everyday speech and idiom.
Throughout the centuries poetry has been written in the language and idiom of the day. Shakespeare didn't insist in writing as Chaucer had before him – why must so many people try and write in ancestral English now-a-days?!

Another every-day uncertainty which faces many an aspiring poet is that of, "I have difficulty knowing where to finish one line and start the next."

Always bear in mind that the layout of any poem should help the reader make sense of what the poet is trying to say. Take three versions of the same first verse of a poem:

gentle fall in pitch. Often used in blank verse (unrhymed iambic pentameter) – a favourite of Shakespeare.

"He was/a scho/lar, and/a ripe/and good/one;

Excee/ding wise,/fair spo/ken, and/persua/ding."

Anacrusis. The use of an extra syllable before the first regular foot of a line.

"Honour/twines a/round her/brows,∧

The jewel/health a/dorns her/neck."

Caesura. This is a pause about the middle of a line, different from that which indicated a dropped syllable. It is usually shown by a pause in the sense.

"The village clock tolled six;/ /I wheeled about"

Although in the majority of cases most of these forms, except those perhaps of rhythmical liberties and syllabic verse, would be used in rhyming forms, this does not necessarily have to follow. You will also find that although it is not necessary to learn the names of the prosodic symbols or types of foot, they will be very useful to you when trying to balance lines in your poems.

Poetry has always been a question of working in the accepted metres and techniques of the day and writing on subjects understandable to the poet's contemporaries. This of course totally contradicts the many aspiring poets who feel that their poetry is not Poetry unless written in the rhyming forms which were learnt (parrot-fashion and mindlessly?) at school or at their mother's knee.

Perhaps the most common of errors found today are the

the second foot appears to have four syllables, but in fact the 'i' of 'Assyrian' is merged with the 'a'. Elision is often shown by an apostrophe, as in stopp'st.

Compensation. Examples of ways of compensating for omissions in a line of metrical verse.

a) A syllable lost in a line may be tacked onto another to repair the loss:

⏑⏑_ ⏑ ⏑ _ ⏑ ⏑ _ ⏑ ⏑ _ ⏑
"To invite/the gods hith/er they would/have had rea/son, →

⏑ _ ⏑ _ ⏑ ⏑ _ ⏑ ⏑ _ ⏑
→And Jove/had descen/ded each night/in the sea/son."

b) However, the compensation usually takes place within the same line:

⏑ _ ⏑ _ ⏑ _ ⏑ ⏑ ⏑ _
"The glance/by day,/the whis/per in the/dark . . ."

with the fourth foot scanned as a tribrach, the extra unstressed syllable there compensating for its omission in the last foot.

c) The use of a pause other than the caesura, such as a 'rest' This is a silence with a temporal value, similar to a rest in music.

"ΛBreak,/Λ break,/Λ break,

At the foot/of thy crags,/O Sea! Λ"

EXTRAMETRICAL SYLLABLES:

Feminine ending. This is an extra unstressed syllable affixed after the final stressed syllable of a line, causing a

4) of a spondaic foot   (— —)

"Tom struts/a sol/dier, o/pen, bold/and brave"

5) of an anapestic foot   (ᴗ ᴗ —)

"And the com/ing wind/did roar/more loud"

Distributed stress. Called 'hovering accent', occurs when it's not obvious which of two consecutive syllables should take the stress.
Example:

"Now came/still Even/ing on,/and twi/light gray . . ."

Dropped syllables. These terms are used for lines that are short of syllables.
Example:

a) Catalectic line – this stops in the middle of the final foot, as in the dactyl line:

"Drunk every/night with a/delicious/tear ∧"

b) Acephalous line – this leaves out the first syllable of the line, as in the anapestic line:

"∧ So no/tions and modes/she referred/to the schools . . ."

Elision. This is the merging of two syllables into one, or the omission of a letter or syllable at the beginning, middle or end of a word. In the anapestic line:

"The Assyr/ian came down/like a wolf/on the fold"

"Yet once more, O ye laurals, and once more, (10 syllables)
Ye myrtles brown with ivy never sere, (10)
I come to pluck your berries harsh and crude." (10)
                                                    Milton

Accentual-syllabic verse demonstrates the improvement in sound when length of syllable (quantity) and metrical accent are made to coincide.
Example:

"The busy world and what you see,

Is all a silly vanity."

METRICAL LICENCES:

Substitution. The use of a foot different from that of the metre in which the poem is written.
Examples: (The effect on iambic verse of some common substitutions).

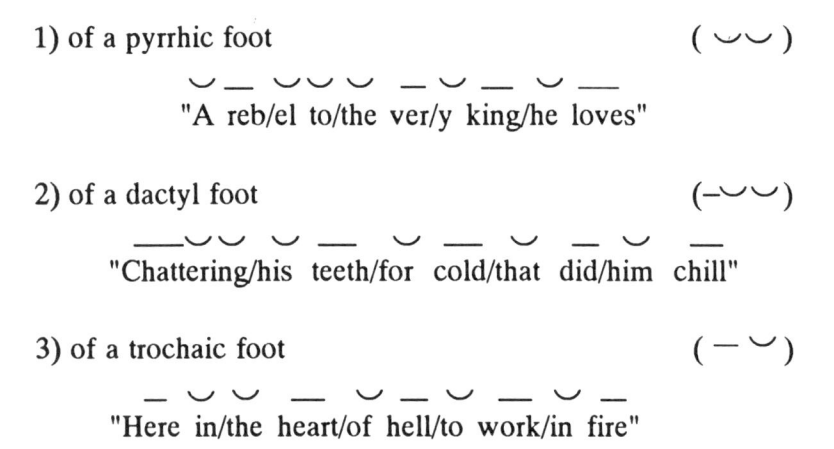

1) of a pyrrhic foot   (⏑⏑)
   "A reb/el to/the ver/y king/he loves"

2) of a dactyl foot   (−⏑⏑)
   "Chattering/his teeth/for cold/that did/him chill"

3) of a trochaic foot   (− ⏑)
   "Here in/the heart/of hell/to work/in fire"

69

Stress Prosody in which both the stresses and syllables are of fixed number.
Example:

"It was no/ drĕam; I lay broad waking;

But all/ is turnĕd, through my gentleness,

Into my strange fashion of forsaking:"

Wyatt

Latin Hexameter. English words arranged on this principle.
Example:

"That to my/advance/ment their/wisdoms/have me a/based

Well may a/pastor/plain; but a/las! his/plaints be not/esteemed/

Oppress'd/with ruin/ous con/ceits by the/aid of an/outcry."

Anon

Syllabic Verse.
Examples:

"Openly, yes (4 syllables)
With the naturalness (6)
Of the hippopotamus or the alligator (13)
When it climbs on the bank to experience the (13)
Sun, I do these (4)
Things which I do, which please (6)
No one but myself. Now I breathe and now I am sub- (13)
merged; the blemishes stand up and shout when the object . . ."
(13)

Moore

Rhythmical Pause
This is not counted as a part of the metrical pattern but is a natural pause which occurs when a reader draws breath between phrases, sometimes creating a sing-song effect in verse with strong rhythm.

METRE:

What is metre? Example of **syncopation** or **counterpoint**
∪ __ ∪ __ ∪ __ ∪ __ ∪ __
"A plain/without/a fea/ture, bare/and brown."   Auden
(read from a *metrical* point if view)

"A plain without a feature, bare and brown."
(read from *word accent* and *stress sense*)

METRICAL SYSTEMS:

Anglo-Saxon Prosody fixed number of stressed syllables, any number of unstressed syllables.
Example:

"And have reuthe on these ribaudes that repent them here sore

That ever thei wratthed the in this world in word

thoughte or dedes."

Langlande

TYPES OF RHYTHM:

Duple Rhythm
Example:
˘ — ˘ — ˘— ˘ —
"His soul/stretched tight/across/the skies."
T S Eliot

Triple Rhythm
Example:
˘ ˘ — ˘ ˘ — ˘ ˘ — ˘ ˘ —
"She is far/from the land/where her young/hero sleeps."
Moore

Rising Rhythm
Where the stress falls on the last syllable of the foot the rhythm is a rising one, as in the last example.

Falling Rhythm
Example:
/ / / /
"Welcome her,/thunders of/fort and of/fleet."
Tennyson

Rocking Rhythm
Example:
/ / / /
"The Bourbon/the Bourbon!/Sans country/or home."
Byron

Running Or Common Rhythm
Where there is an alteration of stressed and unstressed syllables, with a rising or falling duple rhythm we have running or common rhythm.
Example:
/ / / / / / / /
"Ah! Dis/tinctly/I rem/ember,/it was/in the/bleak De/cember."
Poe

Trochee (stressed followed by unstressed syllable).
Example of **trochaic** metre:

— ∪ — ∪ — ∪ — ∪
"Lives of/great men/all re/mind us

— ∪ — ∪ — ∪ —
We can/make our/lives sub/lime . . ."

Anapest (two unstressed followed by a stressed syllable)
Example of **anapestic** metre:

∪ ∪ — ∪ ∪ — ∪ ∪ —
"I am out/of human/ity's reach

∪ ∪ — ∪ ∪ — ∪ ∪ —
I must fin/ish my jour/ney alone . . ."   Cowper

Dactyl (one stressed followed by two unstressed syllables)
Example of **dactylic** metre:

— ∪ ∪ —∪∪
"Make no deep/scrutiny

—∪ ∪ —∪∪
Into her/mutiny

— ∪ ∪ —∪∪
Rash and un/dutiful."   Hood

Other classical feet that occur fairly frequently in verse:

Spondee	— —	two stressed syllables
Pyrrhic	∪ ∪	two unstressed syllables
Amphibrach	∪ — ∪	unstressed/stressed/unstressed
Cretic	— ∪ —	stressed/unstressed/stressed
Tribrach	∪ ∪ ∪	three unstressed syllables
Disyllabic		contains two syllables
Trisyllabic		contains three syllables

Pentameter. Five foot line.
Example:

"Altar wise/by owl-light/in the/half-way/house
The gentle/man lay/graveward/with his/furies."

            Thomas

Hexameter. Six foot line.
Example:

"This is the/forest pri'meval. The/murmuring/
pines and the/hemlocks."

           Longfellow

Heptameter. Seven foot line.
Example:

"There's not/a flower/on all/the hills;/
the frost/is on/the pane."

            Tennyson

Octameter. Eight foot line.
Example:

"Where vir/tue wants/and vice/abounds,/there
wealth/is but/a bait/ed hook . . ."

             Anon

FEET MOST OFTEN USED IN ENGLISH VERSE:

Iamb (unstressed followed by stressed syllable).
Example of **iambic** metre:

  ᴗ _ ᴗ _ ᴗ _ ᴗ _
"O la/dy, twine/no wreath/for me

 ᴗ _ ᴗ _ ᴗ _ ᴗ _
Or twine/it of/the cy/press tree."   Scott

64

CHAPTER VIII

TERMINOLOGY FOR MEASURES:

Monometer. Lines composed of a single foot.
Example:
"Thus I
Passe by,
And die:
As one,
Unknown,
And gon;
Am made
A shade,
And laid
I'th grave."
          Herrick

Dimeter. Two foot line.
Example:
"With rav/ished ears
The mon/arch hears,
Assumes/the god,
Affects/the nod."
          Dryden

Trimeter. Three foot line.
Example:
"Have mer/cey, Lord/on me
As thou/wert ev/er kind."
          Dryden

Tetrameter. Four foot line.
Example:

"By fai/ry hands/their knell/is rung,
By forms/unseen/their dirge/is sung."
          Collins

having fun with a typewriter. And I find that exponents make contradictory statements amongst themselves. On the other hand, Anthony Barnett says: "There is no conclusion to material poetry. As a wide-ranging conscious experiment and investigation into methods of communication and creative work it knows no bounds. This is its fault and its virtue."

I would recommend interested readers to obtain examples of the work of Findlay and Morgan, to see it at its best in English.

* * * *

NB. Howard was kind enough to give this as a talk at one of my poetry get-togethers in the Midlands and I asked him if he would write it down for me. At this point on the original Howard has written in Biro:

Note: For 'he' read 'he or she' throughout. I'm not a male chauvinist pig, but to use both male and female every time would have been confusing.

Bann tells us that the origin dates from 1955 when the German poet Eugen Gomringer and the Brazilian poet--designer Decio Agnitari met in Germany. Both had been experimenting in their respective countries and the meeting gave fresh impetus to their efforts. The movement spread to the UK in the early 60's, where it was taken up in Scotland by Ian Hamilton Finlay and Edwin Morgan who have both produced interesting pieces of work; and in England by Dom Sylvester Houedard and John Furnival.

Why 'Concrete'? To the Brazilians it had something to do with Max Bill's naturalistic painting and sculpture – they issued a manifesto in 1958 in which they stated that a Concrete Poem is an object "in and by itself," in which graphic space is regarded as one of the elements. Gomringer called his poems "constellations." In his *Silencio*

silencio	silencio	silencio
silencio	silencio	silencio
silencio		silencio
silencio	silencio	silencio
silencio	silencio	silencio

one can see how "space" is used at the centre of the piece conveying the message of silence.

For Professor Max Bense the word Concrete is to be understood "in its Hegelian sense." Concrete as the opposite of abstract, because it implies materiality "verbal, vocal or visual."

For Anthony Barnett it is "the material." But I am not writing an essay on the subject, just looking at it from the point of view of the poet. It seems to me that though some of the Concrete efforts can be admired for their ingenuity and skill in word-placing etc, so few of them really have much to say. They concentrate upon the meanings of say a single word in relation to space. Typography and draughtsmanship play their part. Some seem to be simply try it as a musical phrasing emphasising the stressed words and you will find that it works magnificently. One point, Hopkins being complicated as he is, the "level-underneath-him" carries over some of the stress on "level" to the "underneath-him" so that the whole has to be read as a phrase. Modern poets use this form extensively.

CONCRETE POETRY: When it comes to Concrete Poetry we are in another field altogether. Frankly, I think that it is wrongly named. It should be called Multi-Dimensional Poetry (as I called it in an article written early in the Sixties). Stephen Bann, one of the leaders in the UK, wrote about an exhibition at the Lisson Gallery which presented shadows of gently swaying letterist mobiles projected on to a Psychedelic light screen, itself activated by microtonics of Ravi Shankar's music – the exhibition was of Concrete Poetry!

It would seem to me to be an attempt at a fusion or cross-fertilisation of the arts.

It should be noted that Concrete Poetry is not just shaped poetry. George Herbert had poems in shapes which had reference to the subject of the poem, Lewis Carroll has one on a mouse-tail, Appollinaire's *Calligrammes* had poems in shaped sentences, and Dylan Thomas had poems in the shape of diamonds and sandglasses in *Vision and Prayer*. These were not Concrete Poems, but shaped poems, though they may have influenced the development of the idea.

The essential difference lies in the relationship between shape of poem and content. In Concrete Poetry the poem's structure derives from some semantic idea, which may consist of a single word or phrase, presented and represented in different ways. Concrete Poetry seems to have something of graphic design, typography, word-play and anything else the poet might wish to include.

try scanning the first line – it is in fact a three-stress line in sprung rhythm: Stresses:

"<u>Ding</u> <u>Dong</u> <u>Bell</u>
<u>Pussy's</u> <u>in</u> the w<u>e</u>ll
Who put her in?
<u>Li</u>ttle <u>John</u>ny <u>Green</u>"

Gerard Manley Hopkins developed it systematically and elaborately towards the end of the 19th Century. If we decide by this form to use, say, a five stress line, then provided we have five stressed syllables it doesn't matter how many unstressed syllables are included. It is called 'Sprung' rhythm because it has a springing or syncopated effect on the rhythm. Hopkins defined the method rather elaborately and over-extended it, so that his definition tends to be rather difficult to grasp. I think the best way of thinking about it is to see it as the substitution of the musical phrase for the metrical foot. In music the fundamental measure is the bar, but musicians and composers manage to introduce variations by having within each bar some notes which take up the whole of the bar (i.e. one stress) and other notes, indicated by crotchets, quavers and semi-quavers etc which take up other bars, but the time factor is the same. If we see the stresses in the line as the measure, we can introduce shorter notes (i.e. unstressed syllables) as we think fit or rather, as the poem demands. Let us go to Hopkins for our example:

"I ca<u>u</u>ght this mo<u>r</u>ning mo<u>r</u>ning's m<u>i</u>nion, k<u>i</u>ng-

dom of the d<u>a</u>ylight d<u>a</u>uphin, da<u>p</u>ple-dawn-drawn Fa<u>l</u>con, in his ri<u>d</u>ing

Of the ro<u>l</u>ling le<u>v</u>el underneath him st<u>e</u>ady <u>a</u>ir, and str<u>i</u>ding

H<u>ig</u>h there, how he r<u>u</u>ng upon the r<u>e</u>in of a w<u>i</u>mpling w<u>i</u>ng . . ."

Try reading this to a metrical beat and it doesn't work; then

In fact 'free' verse, is free only in the sense that it disregards the traditional disciplines of *rhyme* and *metre*. But if you accept my belief that an essential part of all poetry is that it should organise experience and communicate it by means of a pattern, then you will appreciate that so--called 'free verse' must also have a pattern, though perhaps not so clearly seen as a pattern of rhyme or metre. The pattern may rely on the nature of the content to create the form, or the shape may be dictated by the poem itself, following say natural speech rhythm or the rhythms of the body (we are all subject to a pattern of rhythm – in breathing, in circulation of the blood, in the menstrual pattern of womanhood, in sleep and waking etc).

Walt Whitman used the style throughout his work, though he tended to overdo wordage at times and repeat himself. Perhaps one of the best exponents is Lawrence, particularly in such as poems as *Snake*, and his animal and flower poems. The best poems, it seems to me, have been those in which the pattern approximates to the rhythms of speech. Although many people today choose to write in what they think is 'free verse' because it seems easier than having to find rhymes or work to a metrical pattern, it is in fact <u>far</u> <u>more</u> <u>difficult</u> to write a good poem in this form than in metre or rhyme, simply because some substitute pattern has to be found to replace the heightened impact of the pervasive pattern created by accentual metre. This is what I call 'organic rhythm'.

<u>SPRUNG</u> <u>RHYTHM</u>: This is the attempt to use the actual stressed syllables in a line, rather than metrical feet, as the basic pattern. It was used by many of the early poets for occasional poems, Langland, for instance, and in fact, some of our nursery rhymes use the pattern. If you examine the pattern of *Ding Dong Bell* closely it will be found that it does not actually scan on a metrical basis –

will be seen that the line has ten syllables, arranged in pairs, with one stressed syllable following an unstressed one. In order to avoid monotony a metrical foot can be reversed and this is called counterpoint. Similarly we may use a pattern of iambics, anapests, trochees, dactyls, spondees, etc. All of which have their own stresses.

It will often be found that in addition to the pattern of metrical feet, as shown above, there is also a pattern of natural speech rhythms sometimes working across the metrical pattern and so creating a kind of tension.

BLANK VERSE: This term is often used to refer to all unrhymed verse, but it has generally been restricted to Heroic Verse or Iambic Pentameter. The *only* thing it has in common with Free Verse is that it does not rhyme. It does have a fixed metrical foot. First employed by the Earl of Surrey in the 16th century, it was the metre used by Milton in *Paradise Lost*, by Wordsworth in many of his poems, and by Shakespeare for his plays. Blank Verse, then, usually has ten syllables per line, but lends itself to variations. In this century Blank Verse has been used by Eliot but on a much looser construction. Blank Verse owes its attraction to the fact that it permits better cadence and the absence of rhyme allows the poet to concentrate on language and variations. Vowel and consonantal music, alliteration and assonance can all be used.

FREE VERSE: The term, which comes from the French Vers Libre, is somewhat misleading. It is a contradiction in terms to suggest that Verse or Poetry can be entirely free of all rules, regulations and principles. It is just about the least understood of all forms, and those who simply chop up their writing into long and short lines simply to make them look modern are, in fact, writing prose in long and short lines.

writing, but which I later realised were the essential qualities of the poem.

Poems can be composed in many ways. It may be that a special subject will arouse a line of thought. That lines and phrases which come into the mind set up an interaction of thought and imagery. Or a given image may provide the starting point for the whole poem. Or the poet may even produce his poem in a state of semi-trance as if the words were dictated by some other power (though I do not think this happens very often). Robert Graves says "the nucleus of every poem worthy of the name is rhythmically formed in the poet's mind, during a trance-like suspension of his normal habits of thought, by the supra-logical reconciliation of conflicting emotional ideas. The poet learns to induce the trance in self-protection whenever he feels unable to resolve an emotional conflict by simple logic."

But whatever method is adopted, it is essential that there be some formal organisation of experience – the creation of a pattern. It may be achieved by means of structure, stanzas, images, symbols, paradox, language, metaphor, analogy, parallelism, sound, rhythm, or thoughts, or indeed a combination of these. The really creative genius may even create some new patterns, so that we must always be open to the new and not too dominated by a particular pattern (as those people are who think that all poetry ought to rhyme or be concerned only with "beauty").

It has been necessary for me to explain my position at some length because it influences what I have to say on the subject of Free Verse, Blank Verse, Sprung Rhythm and Concrete Poetry.

The vast majority of poems in English have been written in a pattern of metrical feet on an accentual basis. A metrical foot may consist of two or more syllables according to the accent pattern. For instance, in the Iambic pattern: "When I/ have fears/ that I/ may cease/ to be." it

Human existance as we know it is made up of a whole variety of different experiences. Out of this rich variety of experiences, the poet selects those which seem to him to be significant and re-arranges them to meet his needs; he orders, simplifies and heightens in one way or another, to produce some kind of pattern that is meaningful to others. When I speak of experiences, of course, I include mental and psychological experiences, dream events, imaginative processes, as well as actual physical day-to-day occurrences.

As an editor, critic, and even ordinary reader of poetry, I must have some understanding of the nature of poetry if I am to make valid judgements. As there are no reliable definitions of poetry, I have had to arrive at what I would call a working hypothesis for this purpose, and here it is: "A poem is a selection from the poet's experience which is organised into some kind of pattern, and communicated to an audience/public of one or more." The essentials, then, are (1) A selection from experience (the whole mental, psychological or physical experience – and this includes the books read, music heard, plays seen, poems absorbed etc). (2) Pattern. (3) Communication. Communication for me is important since it completes the creative process. If anyone writes the world's greatest masterpiece and tears it up, or locks it up in the office safe so that no-one else sees it, he has not completed the creative process.

I am not saying that the poet consciously decides on a pattern; quite often the poem decides its own pattern and the poet may not even be aware of it until it is pointed out to him. Several years ago I wrote a 'space poem' for children entitled *Soft Landings*. This has proved to be one of my most successful poems – it has been broadcast and anthologised many times, and a number of editors have critically examined it for their readers, pointing out patterns of creation which I did not realise existed at the time of

If one consults the dictionary one finds: "elevated expression of elevated thought or feeling in metrical form." If I were to start with any one of these every one of my readers could pull it to pieces.

One's recognition of poetry depends upon the recognition of a certain quality, but it seems that no-one can tell us precisely what that quality is in a definition which excludes everything that is *not* poetry and includes everything that *is* poetry.

There are some critics who take a completely subjective view and say that poetry exists only in the individual's response to a piece of writing. That poetry exists only in the mind of the reader or listener. That it is produced by one particular person to fit his own poetic formula, to stimulate himself in such a fashion that it, almost accidentally, affects others also; what Professor Martin once referred to as "the series of events in our minds that for convenience we sometimes all too complacently call poetry." But if that is so, how is it that there is such a marked agreement of opinion amongst readers of all ages and societies, differing only in degree, as to the quality of certain poems written in the past?

Let me make it clear, then, at this point, that while I appreciate that no judgement on poetry can be entirely objective, I do not accept that it is entirely subjective either. From my own experience, I know that if a critic or editor knows his own tastes, prejudices and inclinations well enough he can learn how to discount them in making an assessment of a particular poem or collection of poems, to arrive at a fairly objective judgement. He can therefore like personally a poem which he could criticise as bad, and dislike a poem he could support as of high standard. The best critics, it seems to me, are those who can differentiate between their personal reactions and an objective evaluation. But that is by the way.

CHAPTER VII

A MATTER OF FORM
Some Technical Aspects of Writing Poetry
by
Howard Sergeant MBE

(Reproduced with the kind permission of Jean Sergeant)

I have been asked by Johnathon Clifford to write about form in poetry and in particular to explain Sprung Rhythm, Free Verse, Concrete Poetry etc, and to distinguish between Free Verse and Blank Verse.

However, before I can talk about form in poetry, I am compelled to search for a valid definition of poetry, for I am unable to talk about form in poetry without a knowledge of what poetry is. At this point I run into serious problems, as everyone does who tries to find the perfect definition of poetry. During the past centuries many poets, critics and writers have attempted to define poetry without success. No sooner is a definition formulated than exceptions spring to mind and we can see almost at once that any given definition cannot be strictly confined to poetry. At various times poetry has been described as:

"imitation of human life"
"a glimpse of the divine"
an expression of emotion"
"emotion recollected in tranquility"
"aspiration towards beauty"
"communication of pleasure"

but such definitions tell us nothing about the real nature of poetry.

the same form as 5 or . . . you see what I mean? It isn't so much what you're saying (subject) that controls the shape or form in which a poem must appear, but the emotional content or colour which controls it.

On the following pages there is a talk by Howard Sergeant explaining some of the customary forms, followed by various examples of how they have been used by poets down the ages, many of which are obviously in yesterday's idiom and language.

The interesting exercise is in trying to create similar sound patterns, but in today's language and idiom. It is surprising how helpful it can be to know how the positioning of the words on the page influence the reader's understanding of their emotional content – your basic use of the words' positions as a tool to express what you are trying to achieve through their mere meaning.

In poetry it is often what is said between the words, behind the lines, (the 'words with no sound'), which is important – the overall feel rather than the mechanical words themselves – that gives the essence and bite to your message.

1   Then we were young and matched our strength
    against the stupid senile world,
    and sought to right by argument
    the many problems of our age...

2   Read of vermilion mornings, solitude
    in sunset's rime.
    Read of the stillness, heart-encased
    by the hawk-high silence
    of expectant minds;
    read of the knowledge of the wind,
    dimmed colours found in tiny flowers
    showers and a whirl-wind, pastures and a stone...

    Read of much pain...

3   They say that Doomsday will occur
    at some far distant point in time,
    with floods and tears and great volcanic strife;
    but they are wrong, for Doomsday's been –
    at eight o'clock today, to be precise...

4   I slept and dreamt some vast and hideous army
    stormed my mind as in my sleep I watched
    your progress on along the lemming road
    that you had chosen...

6   "Cash," he said firmly, "is all that is needed,"
    picking his nose with a thoughtful teaspoon –
    stirred in the sugar with great swirling movements
    while humming, quite loudly, an old favourite tune...

7   Now in the Autumn of my life I've found
    a sudden reason why it should be Spring,
    with a blackbird singing in the blue-haze dawn,
    and a primrose flowering...

I have there given you examples from seven different poems. I don't ask you to say whether any of the poems are any good as poetry or could have been said better differently, but what I do ask is that you try and write the emotional content and subject of, say 6, in the same form as 2, or 1 in

CHAPTER VI

WHAT IS POETRY? Isn't it about time we tried to work that out if you are aiming to have a whole book of it!

Everyone who has ever tried to give a definition of poetry in the past has either simply failed; not come up with a description that was valid for all poetry; or was convinced only of the uncertainty and unsure footing of his definition.

However, I shall not plead the coward and shy away from having a stab at the same problem. Poetry is . . . er . . . um . . . (hang on a minute while I put my teeth in) . . .

"Poetry is a disciplined collection of words which, by its controlled sound pattern, shape on page, or combination of both, cannot be prose."

That is, I believe, the nearest I can get to it, though as a 'negative definition' it leaves much to be desired and no doubt as every one of you read that, you will find examples with which to shoot it down. But everyone else has had a stab at it, so now – so have I!

Personally I really believe that to describe what poetry is, rather than is not, is an impossible task.

It is surprising (to me anyway) how many people try to write every single one of their poems in the same basic form. Every single subject from the uproariously boisterously happy, to the miserably macabre – how *can* it work?

It can be quite rightly argued that a poem will 'find its own form' and invariably there are almost as many poetic forms as there are subjects, or rather, as there are different emotional approaches to a subject. Let me try and explain this with a few examples:

chances of your getting four entries from a high percentage of your entrants is correspondingly better.

Also bear in mind you must keep extremely accurate records of all entrants and sums of money – open a separate bank account for your competition. You *must* be able to demonstrate the probity of your competition on request

I've also found that poets like to have a chance of getting *something* from the competition, if not a cash prize. It therefore pays dividends to have an anthology of say, the best 30 or 50 poems entered, for sale at say £2 a copy (order when entering, makes life more simple for the organisers) in which the winning poems, the judge's deliberations and a list of Highly Commendeds will appear. And for heaven's sake make sure that the anthology is *well* produced – not cheap, tatty and full of typesetting errors. Remember, you want your entrants to be straining at the leash to enter again next year!

Make sure that the flyer you have printed about your competition – the organ that will advertise it for you, contains all the necessary information – rules, the judges and who they are, closing date, intended date of announcement of winners (always ask for an s.a.e. for the return of entries and notification of results) and the statement that 'the judge's decision is final'.

If you are running your competition in aid of a charity there is a good chance that some of the Women's magazines will be willing to give it coverage for you – but only if you remember how far ahead they work and give their Features Editor full details some *four to six months* in advance.

involved with (to feel a part of) the group of which they have become a member. You need a Press Relations person (if no others) – don't try and do everything yourself, it won't work and the others will feel 'left out'.

Arrange that a report of each meeting is sent to the local press with details such as who attended, what was done, what and when the next meeting is to be. Build up a rapport with your local Press, for it is through them you will attract new blood and hopefully involve your group with the local community by giving poetry recitals for your local homes and hospices – to name just two possibilities.

You can also raise funds for your group or for some local charity of your choice, by organising local or national

POETRY COMPETITIONS: Every year over a period of some five years (ending in 1988 when I raised over £6,000 for the *International Musicians Seminar*) I organised a national poetry competition in aid of a different charity. Since then the work load of the NPF has made it impossible to continue with these, though as Trustees, we do judge external competitions, free of charge.

During those years I gained quite an insight into what it was that the entrants wanted of their competitions and the judges.

The rules for your competition must be as open as possible. Don't restrict entries with some inane line limitation. Don't debar poems that have been published before or entered for a previous competition or been accepted for publication – allow *"any number of entries on any subject or length, whether published before or not."*

Make sure that the fee you charge is fair and not excessive. However high the prize money an unrealistic entry fee will put off many potential entrants. If you have an entry fee of £2 for the first poem and £1 per poem thereafter it does divide rather simply into five, and the of one's school days – one's childhood – especially as one gets older) becomes more entrenched in the memory, more fondly remembered. Most of the older generation were taught to learn by rote – learning tables and then as a group chanting them in class – "six eights are forty-eight, seven eights are fifty-six, eight eights are sixty . . . er . . . um; hang on Sir, it'll come to me!" Well I never was very good at sums . . .

"Amo, amas, amat . . . " Great swathes of poems to be repeated, recited, rehearsed aloud in front of class. It is not really surprising, then, that such learning was impressed on the mind as the yardstick of excellence. Like the poetry or not, learnt in that fashion it was a form of brain-washing.

But all that aside, setting up your own poetry group or society (now you have been warned of the worst you can expect!) can be a most satisfactory way in which to involve yourself with other poets. So how can you go about

<u>SETTING UP A POETRY GROUP</u>: Almost certainly there'll already be a group in your area so you must have a very clear idea of exactly what it is you want *your* group to achieve. Have a *clear* idea of the sort of format that your meetings are to have, and why.

First find somewhere you can meet on a regular basis – the same evening each month at the same time – then contact your local newspaper and radio and ask them to give publicity to your venture. It is here that you state your aims and announce the time and date of your first meeting. At the end of each meeting be certain everyone's aware of the agenda and date of the next.

It is imperative that you achieve a balance between leading, and involving, those who join. The very fact that they have come to join your group, means they wish someone else to initiate organisation, but most prefer to be bitterness and vilification of yours truly, to start their own very short-lived - group).

Subsequently I learned that Howard Sergeant had tried setting up something rather similar to area branches in the late 40's, with much the same end result. It would seem people are often quick to cry for constructive criticism, when what they really seek is undiluted and meaningless praise. Oh fair enough! That is far too sweeping a statement. Let me re-phrase it . . . the better the poet, the more open she or he is to discussion around their poetry, sensible to the fact that such discussion can only be useful to their development as a poet.

The more inept the poets, the more convinced they are of the god-given brilliance of what they write and nine-times-out-of-ten, will hear not even the mildest word of criticism of it - however constructive or well-meant.

Arm-in-arm may also be found the 'if-it-doesn't-rhyme-it-isn't-poetry' league of the poetically blind and those who avow they've "no time for modern poetry." Oh dear!

There is no such thing as modern poetry; there is poetry that is written today; there is poetry that was written yesterday; there is poetry that will be written tomorrow; but modern poetry? All poetry is, will be and was, modern poetry.

Chaucer was the modern poet of his day; Shakespeare of his; Wordsworth of his; and so it will go on. Poetry has throughout the centuries been written in the language and idiom of the day and the fact that you admire and enjoy what was written a hundred or more years ago doesn't mean that is the language in which you should be writing today (whether it rhymes or not), any more than Wordsworth should have tried to ape Shakespeare, or Shakespeare, Chaucer.

In many instances what one was taught (what was a part

CHAPTER V

As I have said previously, back in the early 70's I organised workshops in my area and found that most of those who attended thoroughly enjoyed them, turning up as regular as clockwork every month. Encouraged by this local enthusiasm I organised four

LOCAL BRANCHES in England where, supplied by a central office with homework, exercise pieces, visiting readings by members from other parts of the country, and occasional visits by me, members of a local group could benefit from being a part of a national organisation.

Initially these first four branches (Coventry, Bicester, St. Helens and Bath) worked efficiently, though once some found there were no glorified self-congratulatory evenings and that a discipline of work was expected, they dropped away. As did the odd middle-aged Harridan who had been used to lording it over some previous club. You all no doubt recognise her – of that 'indiscriminate' age, strident-voiced, self-opinionated, of the firm belief that the only voice, opinion and poetry worth listening to is her own – there seems to be one such in most societies!

Then there was the branch that worked magnificently, until the director decided to take it over and turn it into a local society of his own.

I'm sure all the branches could have worked. The theory was there, but somehow *people* made sure they didn't (work, I mean) and I found I was spending more time sorting out local wrangles than concentrating on poetry. (I even experienced problems with my own local branch where a minority thought they *were* the organisation, rather than the less-than-a-tenth-of-it, as was in fact the case. A group of them broke away with some rancour, a Consultant Geriatrician for Portsmouth and Gosport.

Apart from the fact that all decisions materially affecting the running of the NPF have to have been discussed, agreed and minuted at a Trustees' meeting, we also have to produce an annual financial report for the Charity Commissioners which proves beyond doubt that our funds are used for the purpose they are intended. A registered charity is therefore answerable, not to some vague and unwritten agreement, or some cobbled and hardly remembered document, but In Law.

feel all genuine magazine editors, who foresee what they have set up continuing after them, must take into consideration. The only way to make sure that there is some chance of a continuum is to get someone in to help edit the magazine/run the organisation at quite an early stage in its career (hopefully someone half the founder's age). That way someone else is steeped in the original aims of the magazine or organisation.

Our Charter states that: "*there shall be no fewer than three (3) and no more than five (5) Trustees at any one time, though others with specific abilities may be co-opted from time to time if and when it may be felt necessary.*"

Helen Robinson became a member of the poetry service organisation I ran in 1978. She was awarded the Martha Lilian Award for *The Most Promising Young Poet of the Year* in 1979 when it was judged by Howard Sergeant MBE and subsequently went off to Lancaster University where she gained a 1st Class Hons Degree in Engineering. She then became a Trustee of the Foundation and has since been involved with the typesetting of books, judging competitions, helping at recitals and in all the other more humdrum and trivial day-to-day activities of the NPF, and now is the editor of PAUSE.

She knows the aims and direction of the NPF as well as I and being only in her early thirties - against my present (remarkably young!) 53 - will take over as Senior Trustee after me, and the Foundation will continue very much as it has. "*A good manager is one who has so organised his department that should he drop dead the department will continue to function as though he is still there - without the slightest hiccup.*" That was something I was taught in my training as a Production Manager, and something I have tried to bring to the NPF.

Apart from myself the other person who currently makes up the Board of Trustees, is **Dr Althea Lord** who is had created – there was still room for your own 'hand on the tiller' but not to the extent of erasing totally what Howard had so painstakingly built over such a long period . . .

Roland replied;

Dear Johnathon,

5. x. 1993

. . . Since inheriting Outposts I have more than doubled the subscription list, but lost about 600 during the recession . . . the position has been difficult for the last two years – but now the list is growing again with 69 new/returned subscribers in the last six weeks . . .
. . . Of course there are financial problems. It costs a fair amount of money to print the magazine and make a small payment to the contributors – unlike the major magazines that are Outposts rivals it does not receive a five figure grant (PN Review £18,000, Agenda £13,600, Poetry Review £34,000, London Magazine £22,600), nor does the Arts Council pay me a salary . . . Get your facts right before pretending to be indignant!

Best wishes
Roland John
HIPPOPOTAMUS PRESS

– it would appear that Outposts no longer has the identity of its own letterhead.

Two magazines taken forward by new editors, two completely different results – the one successful, the other (inherited in very different circumstances) rather a disaster for those who respected what Howard had created and wanted to see it survive. Both editors doing everything they did from the most honest of motives.

Where the Foundation is concerned all such problems have been eliminated by it being a registered charity with a Charter which governs what the Trustees may and may not do, so it is only 'within tramlines' that after my death or retirement the aims of what I set out originally can be changed – for better or for worse! But this is something I

In the case of Howard Sergeant's *Outposts* we have a very different situation. A very difficult situation for Roland John who took over the editorship on Howard's death. Howard had set up *Outposts* in 1943 and had, until 1987, run it single-handedly both in day-to-day workload and in vision and direction – it had become the prime example of a magazine and its stewardship, and the oldest magazine under the same editorship.

To take over such was a heavy responsibility indeed. I feel I can best illustrate what has happened in *Outposts'* case, by quoting part of a letter I wrote to Roland recently when reminded that my annual sub' was due for renewal. I mean no disrespect to Roland in any way; only that I feel in the direction he took with *Outposts* he failed to understand what he had inherited. This does not mean I feel *Outposts* to be a lesser magazine than it was, only that it is so totally different from that which Howard set up that it should alter its name to reflect so radical a change:

15th Sept 1993

Dear Roland,

... Initially my subscription to OUTPOSTS was because I had always very much enjoyed it as a magazine and because of my friendship with Howard – but during the last few issues it has become less and less poetry with which I could associate. This issue is a good example – some good poetry, much work that seems to lack any rationale for its publication. If it is of any help to you, during the last few months I have had many comments about OUTPOSTS thrust at me:
"It has become too narrow."
"I didn't recognise it as OUTPOSTS any more so I stopped subscribing."
"What is Roland trying to do? He's lost me!"

... and many more, equally as negative.

Perhaps it is a question that taking over a magazine of such weight should have called for a keeping of it within the bounds that Howard *many people* have written for grants to publish their book, or to do the thousand and one things that are not remotely poetry orientated! Unfortunately we cannot even start to consider them as they fall outside our mandate. But then we can't support everything from a very limited budget.

I feel I should stress that there is no imperative that demands we give away the money we raise from these recitals (some £5,000+ to date). We could equally keep it for the Foundation's own benefit – but how much more good it does by spreading it around a little!

Continuance: I have always felt (and it has been borne out from the example of others) that if one has set up something of value, whether that be simply a magazine, or an organisation, then it is important that it doesn't lapse or lose direction with one's own retirement or death.

Two contrasting examples (I believe) are provided by *Envoi* and *Outposts*.

When Roger Elkin took over *Envoi* from its twelve year editorship by Anne Lewis-Smith it was felt by some to have become, under her stewardship, rather a 'comfy magazine which didn't stretch its membership', or (if you will) a 'club' which once one had become a member, would not fail to represent you within its pages – personally I felt that an unfair comment and that Anne had given her all during her twelve year stint, but I am not here reporting a personal opinion, only the grapevine tittle-tattle.

Roger Elkin very quickly imposed his hand on *Envoi's* tiller and, with the putting out of one or two nose-joints, strengthened the magazine's reputation amongst poets.

Let me quickly hasten to add, there is no sense of right or wrong. Anne Lewis-Smith saw the direction of *Envoi* in one light, Roger Elkin in another – both valid for their subscribers at the time, but the one poetically somewhat stronger than the other.

new address and the fact that one of Mark's publications (*Seeing's Believing* by Helen Kitson) had been shortlisted for The Forward Poetry Prize (1993) *Best First Collection* with a prize of £5,000 and that all four poems he had entered on behalf of clients for the *Best Individual Poem* (£1,000 prize) had reached the anthology from which the winners are chosen. Would Mark have been able to continue with his publications, but for our help? Would this success have come about? I like to think that both answers would be "Yes," because I'm sure that anyone destined to do anything worthwhile in any sphere will do it in spite of everything, but it is still warming to think . . . we gave Mark his grant.

Here are just some examples of our grant aid scheme – judge its value from these, which are but a few of the many.

From *my* original rush to support anything that moved, *we* have become wiser and now very carefully vet any request. Of course as a Registered Charity we have tight constraints where what we can and can't support are concerned.

When I originally wrote the Foundation's Charter I not only wrote in the safeguard that "no Trustee, past or present, nor friend or relative of such a Trustee may benefit in any way from the Foundation or its services," I also wanted to leave what we could do as open as possible, and so stated our official registered function as being:

" **for the furtherance of poetry in the UK.**"

Within that definition, I thought, we can handle most things – other than of course giving a grant to someone to publish their book (we publish books if we feel the work is good enough, if we don't feel it is we wouldn't publish it anyway, so we wouldn't give such an applicant a grant – coals to Newcastle, as it were!) . . . You tell me *just how* "in the English language!"

Early in 1991 Josephine Austin of *First Time* magazine rang me to say the Arts Council had turned down her application for a £500 grant on the grounds that "it was too small an amount to administer" (I quote their letter). In view of the fact that she had been running her magazine for some twelve years single-handed, through illness and in health, and that although the overall standard was not high, many people first published in *First Time* had gone on to greater things in magazines of a higher standing in the poetry world, we felt it more than warranted financial help and gave it £500 in February 1991. Although we were not able to ascertain to what extent our grant had been of value, or in what way it had been used, we pressed on . . . the next applicant was Dr Mario Petrucci who contacted us from Enfield asking our support for *The Bound Spiral*, which we were pleased to give. Since then Mario has kept in touch with us and his magazine has gone from strength to strength – good poetry, good reviews, an original and interesting layout – money well spent from our point of view, and a magazine worth supporting. For those who'd like proof of the pudding, his address is in the list of magazines at the back of this book.

We followed that with a grant to help pay for another magazine's replacement roneo machine, and that with a grant to an individual who had been badly let down by a major bookshop.

Scratch magazine is another real success story as far as our scheme is concerned. Again, a small grant was applied for, which we were happy to provide.

For months we heard nothing, apart from the fact that Mark Robinson had moved with no apparent forwarding address! We thought *Scratch* had gone the way of all mirages and our grant money with it! – but no, lo-and-behold, a month or so ago I was given news of *Scratch* at its

I realised that to get the idea off the ground I would need a 'Name' to carry the first performance so contacted Spike Milligan (subsequently awarded the CBE) and asked him if he would be prepared to lend his name to our efforts – not only did he agree, but both he and Beryl Reid OBE graced our first performance at Chiswick in October 1990. The audience were wonderful and we raised £840 from the evening.

Subsequently we performed at Haywards Heath, Enfield (three times) where Susan Penhaligon – a fine poet in her own right – joined us, and at East Grinstead.

So far not only have we been able to give grant aid to seven magazines as far afield as Hastings, Bradford, York and London, but also to give financial help to two individuals, one in Hull and one in the West Midlands. The recitals of themselves have also provided a wonderful extension of the outlets for the poetry of those NPF subscribers who have had books published with us, for it is in the main such poetry that each actor and actress uses for their individual programme.

Since Spike Milligan's triple heart bypass operation in September of '93 the recitals have been on hold, though we are hopeful of restarting them again shortly.

GRANTS: Not that anyone should (or ever would) seek 'grovelling thanks' for being able and willing to supply grant aid, but if those who have been only too happy to receive such help will simply acknowledge the fact in their magazine, then that has always been enough.

So how did those we have so far supported react, and what effect has that reaction had on our thoughts where further grants are concerned?

One of our first applicants was a Welsh magazine which requested £25,000 to top up the grants it already received elsewhere – we pointed out that we only supported poetry with funds and that they may have to wait (a couple of months!) before they'll see their book, is profoundly amusing to say the least – and then they ask about 'their royalties', forgetting that the whole reason the large publishers shy away from taking up a unknown poet is exactly because no money can be made, no profit for either them (the publisher), or the poet.

We've had another occurrence – not so amusing – the poet who (and this happened) failed an exam and then tried to blame us for causing her undue stress in that we hadn't produced her book as quickly as she thought we would . . . thus causing her (would you believe) to fail!

The other approach which is hurtful (if you allow it to be) is the idiot who accuses the NPF of being Vanity Press – normally levelled by a magazine editor who has no real idea of what we do, doesn't publish books for his subscribers and wouldn't know where to start if he was asked to. So such remarks, difficult though it is, have to be accepted with a great deal of charity.

RECITALS: In 1991 I decided that there was a necessity for someone to act as a long-stop for those worthwhile outlets in the poetry world which, although offering a genuine service for poets and poetry, weren't able to command support from the grant-making agencies. But how to get into a situation of being able to supply such funding? Recitals perhaps?

I got in touch with EQUITY who were kind enough to put an item in their magazine, *The Stage,* to the effect that I was looking for actors and actresses who would take part in poetry recitals in aid of charity. I was happily surprised to have an immediate response from Malindi O'Rorke, Jenny Rowan and Dawn Alleyn, all of whom, enthusiastic about the idea, joined me and with Mimi Gale and Desmond Tyler formed the initial group.

THE ROSEMARY ARTHUR AWARD (1989)

This is an annual award decided on February 3rd each year and is open to anyone living in the U.K. The winner receives:

The funding of a perfectly bound book of their poetry

A suitably inscribed carriage clock

£100 in cash

To be eligible for the award the entrant must not previously have had a book published nor published one of their own work themselves and must be a permanent resident in the U.K.

Before December 31st each year the entrant must send 40 poems (none of which must have any means of identification on them) together with a separate sheet with their name, address and acknowledgements (if any); a £5 reading fee; a declaration that they have not had a previous book; and a suitably stamped envelope for notification of the winner and return of poems to:

The National Poetry Foundation
27 Mill Road
Fareham
Hants
PO16 0TH

Previous winners' books available on application to the NPF.

have been able to progress to properly illustrated covers. This is also in no small part thanks to the industry and photographic prowess of Celia Rambaut of Bosley. Celia had for many years taken black-and-white photos, not just of the area around her (in the Peak District) but also whenever she was on holiday. Thus she has a wonderful collection of landscapes, gardens and other interesting natural settings, all and any of which we are able to use – Celia processing the photos so that they are suitable for A5 covers – at no cost to the NPF.

It is only because of the extreme generosity of Rosemary, and the hard work and dedication to the NPF of Celia Rambaut that, not only have we had many fine reviews for our books in the various poetry magazines, but also in such magazines as *Choice, Farmers Weekly, The Engineer* and many of the women's magazines and also on radio, TV and in the local Press (whenever there is a fee available, this goes to the poet, never to the NPF). For however good the poet and the poetry, if the book is small and insignificant, the poet will not be given the acclaim he or she deserves.

One thing that I have to admit does amuse me about the publication of books for people is their inability (in so many cases) to appreciate what is involved financially. We charge an annual reading fee, which does no more than pay for the day-to-day running of the NPF – the letterheads, telephone, postage and occasional transport. It has nothing to do with the cost involved in the publication of each book (which is paid for by Rosemary, sales of books, and other donations we receive) – they cost on average some £600 *each*, and that is with us doing our own typesetting for which we do not charge. Yet it will never cease to surprise me how many poets seem to think that we (or any other publisher for that matter) have a bottomless money-well from which to draw funds – the disbelief and even (in some instances) anger when one is told that we have to be careful

The aims were, and still are: To publish books of peoples' poetry (where the standard of their work is felt to be high enough) at no charge to the poet concerned.

To produce a magazine bi-annually in which to highlight the best of the submitted poetry and also to use it as a newsletter.

To give advice about poetry – without pulling any punches and with no fear nor favour – where it is not felt to be up to standard, and where it was, try to help that poet get further recognition.

To make sure that everyone receives an answer to queries, or evaluation on their poetry, within the shortest of time spans and to carry information and advertising for other organisations free of charge.

Progress: We published our first booklet *Church Bells On A Wet Sunday* by Deirdre Armes Smith – a slim, 17 page affair – in 1986, and subsequently published 20 similar booklets over the next three years.

It was at this point that we were blest (the only really apt word) to find what Howard Sergeant had always insisted I should need to search for in view of my disbelief in the Established funding agencies – a Fairy Godmother with her financial wand. She appeared in the form of Rosemary Arthur. It is only thanks to Rosemary's financial support that we have been able to upgrade our publications from very slim stapled booklets with plain colour covers, to 40/50 page perfectly bound books, with fine illustrated covers.

Rosemary also had the foresight to set up and Covenant The Rosemary Arthur Award which she was kind enough to ask us, the NPF Trustees, to administer. This is a unique annual award for a poet who has not previously had a book of work published (see page 35).

I mentioned that thanks to Rosemary's financial help we

awaiting some money to be cleared through the Bank of Canada for her, and would pay her bill when that was through.

At the get-together a business man stated that he was to give an annual £500 donation to my work (he died of a heart attack two weeks later) and she (*my* Contessa!) that she would organise with her attorney to make an annual donation of $3,000 to the same cause. You can imagine how much I felt I had 'arrived'.

A week after the get-together week-end the hotel rang me to ask what I intended to do about the Contessa – she was still there, still ringing up her bill, especially when the bar was open! When asked to make some token payment, or small inroad into her indebtedness to the hotel she had simply told them she had no money . . . and left! The hotel (quite rightly in the circumstances – I had not covered myself as get-together organiser) held me responsible for her £1,500 bill –*fifteen hundred pounds.* To say that the payment of that bill wiped me and my poetry service out would be an understatement, to say it almost caused my already doubtful health to completely collapse would be nearer the truth. It took me two years to get over the emotional and financial blow.

But – let nothing happen from which we do not learn – a very much wiser person, I took what had been of value in my poetry service, PAUSE amongst others and, with further advice from Howard and Sir John, wrote the Charter of the National Poetry Foundation, applying and succeeding in getting it registered as a charity in early 1981.

The first two names to give donations to the new NPF were Sir John Betjeman and Lord Ted Willis (who subsequently became a Patron). Since then it has gone from strength to strength.

and 'bureaucracy' in the Poetry World; fed up with the Arts Council's every-few-year-threat to remove or withhold the Poetry Society's grant and control that body's apparent excesses and managerial stupidities without actually ever doing so; fed up with 'closed-shop' publishing outlets, where some editors seemed bent on publishing *only* their own poetry and that of their friends. (Things have improved since the early 70's although the approximately five year round between the Arts Council and the Poetry Society is with us again at the time of writing – see page 93).

So what was needed? An organisation which would look at anybody's poetry and reply straight away. An outlet that would publish books of poetry at no cost to the poet concerned and with no favour to any individual. An organisation where those running it were *unable* to use its funds or services to their own or their friends' benefit – in short, what should have existed from the start of mass communication early this century.

In February 1976 we created the first copy of PAUSE (I say 'we' because I had that year started a poetry service with local branches in different towns in England) which was an orange loose-leaf binder containing twenty A4 typed pages of poetry by Sue Pearson, Arthur Jackson, Shirley Johnston, W J Worthington and Janet Stewart, edited by myself – I'm sure of my facts as I have the only copy left of that first issue in front of me as I write. Now, PAUSE as the vehicle of the National Poetry Foundation, is a perfectly bound 50-plus page book in its 40th edition.

Throughout the late 70's I ran this poetry service (with its branches in various towns) and an annual get-together for poets at a Midland hotel, which became very popular – so popular in fact that I had a real live Contessa apply to attend, all the way from Spain! You can imagine how impressed I was! She duly arrived almost a week before the get-together was due to take place saying that she was

I'm sure it was the involvement with other writers, as much as my boredom with life, that made me write a full length play all in metre, pick a cast, rehearse it, produce it, direct it, and get someone to write some original music for it. This I put on at the local town hall/theatre one Friday evening . . . it poured with rain and there was something (quite what escapes my memory, *Gone With The Wind*, again perhaps?) on TV which meant the audience was rather small, but I have to say – they loved it! It consequently later that year (1973) went on to win the Herringshaw Trophy for the Best Original Play at the Birmingham Theatre Festival.

No-one could have been more surprised than I at the response. I was invited onto local radio and TV; I was invited onto National TV and HTV; I was invited onto most of the local radio stations throughout the UK; I was invited to various theatres (mainly in the Midlands) to read and talk about my poetry; but *most* surprising was the continual flood of letters I received – the continual complaint that "there are no services for the aspiring poet in the UK."

So I decided to look into what was available and, after some four years (using techniques I had mastered as a Production Manager) had to admit that in the majority of cases it wasn't a question of sour grapes by rejected poets, but that something seemed genuinely 'missing' – what?

It was during this search of mine that I had the pleasure to meet both Howard Sergeant MBE and Sir John Betjeman (both unfortunately no longer with us) and it was with them that I discussed the problems. It seemed that what 'services' there were, were very much limited to London and the South East. Poets were fed up with touchy egos and small cliques (the 'gangs' of my title!) in the poetry world; the wrangling, the in-fighting, the squabbling in the poetry hierarchy; fed up with having to wait months to hear anything about submitted work; fed up with 'facelessness'

CHAPTER IV

THE NATIONAL POETRY FOUNDATION: As everyone always says (because it is normally true) I had written poetry "from a very early age." (10ish, in my case). But something that is perhaps slightly more unusual is the fact that I can remember the first poem I ever wrote (being, at the time, heavily into newly-found Shakespeare):

> Men are but children of a larger growth,
> the mental stature warrants not the extra size,
> they laugh to scorn the man
> who through his sense reveres the butterfly
> but fill their lives with senseless thing
> – the thoughts of woman.

Yes, after being adopted at two-and-a-half, sent to boarding school at three-and-a-half, you could argue that I was a somewhat strange, somewhat lonely child.

But enough of my childhood . . . some years later (in 1966) I was involved in an horrendous car accident where I was at the wrong end of a drunk in a large car who killed my passenger and left me with most of my bones broken and in a coma for months. "He'll not come round!" was what the (conscious) members of my family were informed – I did – "You'll not walk again," I was told. It took me three and a half years to learn to play badminton.

During this time (apart from finding my feet again) I had little else to do but concentrate on writing poetry and, more important, on being involved with other poets. In 1971 I set up a small group called Workshop '71 which met in the local church hall to discuss each others' poems and try to find outlets for them. It was with this group that I gained my first experience of organising and taking part in recitals – mainly at local OAP and handicapped peoples' homes.

personally lost touch with it, *Acumen* is another magazine which is more than worthy of your attention.

Once you have had work accepted by established poetry magazines over a period, you may then wish to approach one of the many

SMALL PUBLISHING HOUSES: with a view to their taking up your poetry and publishing a book. This will be governed (depending on the House you choose) by many imponderables . . . does the House have any funds available, is a starter few people think of. Does your work fit with the House's established criteria for acceptance? Do you live in the right part of the country? Are you of the right ethnic group? Are you related to the editor? etc, etc, and finally . . . is your poetry any good? (You will notice that with a few of the smaller, less established Houses, there are questions asked which should have not the slightest priority, while the *important* question is the last asked!).

Quite seriously though, you have to bear in mind that there is *precious little funding for poetry* - ever - and always more poets looking for a publisher, than publishers with funds, so it may well be at this stage you will complete the circle by returning to the bottom of page 16, or have to find some other means of publication.

value to poetry doesn't exist. Where poetry is concerned what is written in the two main reference works leaves out much, but of the two the best is The Writers Handbook, ISBN 0-333-59955-1, edited by Barry Turner and published by Macmillan.

You should remember that it is difficult for reference works to keep track of which magazines still exist and which have just sprung up, only to disappear again as suddenly. It is therefore somewhat a hit-and-miss process to find those in which it is of value to be seen.

All you can do is to write to as many magazines as you can afford, asking them to sell you a back number so that you may judge whether what you write fits with what they publish, or, if what they publish is poetry of any standard, or none at all!

Of the magazines I have experienced I would suggest *Acumen, The Bound Spiral, Envoi, Iota, Iron, Orbis, Outposts, The Poetry Review* and *Scratch* (in no significant, other than alphabetical, order – their addresses appear in the list of magazines at the end of the book). *The Bound Spiral* and *Scratch* are mentioned elsewhere. *Iron*, as its name implies, gives the impression of being North Country, though it publishes work from any area and has one of the most equitable Letters Pages to be found in any magazine with, it would appear, not a jot of editorial bias. *Orbis* is another well-produced magazine that organises and sponsors an annual *Rhyme Revival* Competition which is to be admired and supported. Its editor used also to run weekend workshops which I feel should, if possible, be revived. *Outposts,* though not being the *Outposts* I remember when edited by Howard Sergeant MBE, is still a fine magazine (though personally I feel it should be renamed to take account of its new editorial policy). *Iota* is another fine, though lesser-league magazine, while *The Poetry Review* is also mentioned elsewhere. And although I have

<u>Copyright Copies</u>: By law, copies of every book published in the United Kingdom must be sent to the Copyright Receipt Offices – one (1) copy of your book must go to:

> The Legal Deposit Office
> The British Library
> Boston Spa
> Wetherby
> West Yorkshire
> LS23 7BY

and five (5) copies to:

> Copyright Receipts Office
> 100 Euston Street
> London NW1 2HQ

(who distribute them to the major University Libraries throughout the UK).

NB. *It is your responsibility as publisher to send out the required copyright copies.*

Really I'm again jumping the gun – better you have gone through the more normal channels of seeing your poems in print alongside those of other poets before trying to publish a book of your work. For such exposure you need the

<u>POETRY MAGAZINES</u> which not only let the poetry market come to know your work, but also allow you to learn your trade and judge the quality of what you have to offer against what is being written by others.

A complete list of all the many magazines and their

First Poem

(make sure that all your poems are typeset in the same font and have a standard layout, and that the typeface you use is large enough to be easily read)

Dedication
(which should be short
and to
the point)

CONTENTS

Name Of Poem 1
Name Of Poem 2
Name Of Poem 3

© Name of Author, year of publication

Sponsored by   (if there is a sponsor)

Cover photograph/drawing etc by (if there is one)

Edited by (name of your editor)

Poetry previously published in . . .

All rights reserved. No part of this publication may be reproduced, stored on a retrieval system, or transmitted, in any form or by any means, without prior permission of the publisher.

ISBN number . . .

TITLE

by

Author

Published by
Name
Address

Printed by
Name
Address

Offices (listed on page 26).

Once your chosen Printer has typeset your book you <u>must</u> make sure you are given a 'proof copy' *before* he goes ahead with the printing so that you may

<u>Proof Read</u> your publication. This is one of the most difficult of arts though many people claim to have their own foolproof way of doing it. Perhaps the best way for the inexperienced is to read each page from the bottom up, this way what you are reading doesn't make sense and your eye is less likely to read what your brain tells you *should* be there, rather than what is! Another useful way is to read it aloud (including punctuation and line and verse ends) to a friend who cross checks with the original – though this is a labour-intensive scheme and should be accompanied by plenty of tea breaks or rests. But check . . . check . . . check . . . and then double check again!

Once you've proof read your ms, why not get someone else to cast their eye over it as well?

Never hurry proof-reading. When your book's published you cannot change or correct anything!

Let me give you a salutory example from my own experience:

Many years ago one of my poems was to appear in an anthology which a friend and his wife had compiled. It was to be my first published poem. A poem that had the word Owl in the title. I was to help proof-read . . . I proof-read, he proof-read, she proof-read – we all proof-read together – and his Printer then cast his experienced eye over the ready-to-be-printed ms. Some weeks later we each received our lovingly produced anthology – the word Owl in the title of my poem was spelt Wol. I was heart-broken. So be warned, proof-reading is not to be lightly undertaken!

Now you have your printed and published book in your hand, what do you do with it? First and foremost:

your dedication with the following facing page being the first of your poems.

General Layout: It always looks better if you have only one poem per page (however short) and have each page with the same basic layout. Remember when choosing the type face and point (size of print) that it should be large enough for normally-sighted people to be able to read easily without glasses. Keep away from having twiddly and over-ornate wiggly bits (great swathes of columbine-like flowers decorating your pages or cover). It is fussy, Victorian, and usually annoying to the eye.

You also need to bear in mind (and this depends on how much money you have to spare) that a book needs to appear substantial – in other words if you want to see your books sell, don't rush into print the minute you have twenty poems together and produce an anorexic book, wait until you have a minimum of forty or so, then your book will be a weighty enough tome. If it is to attract the interest of bookshops you will need to have a proper spine (you can't have that without the 40ish minimum number of poems) with the book's details upon it – author and title. You also should have a small photo of yourself on the back cover (all helps to make your book 'reader-friendly') – make sure this is as flattering as your features will allow, make it head-and-shoulders (not you and auntie and uncle at the carnival) and make sure there are no floral tributes growing out of the back of your head (be careful what you're standing in front of!) – with your CV, the price and your bar code.

But all this, as I said, depends really on how much money you have to spend on your book, and if it is for no-one other than your friends and family it does not need to be other than a small stapled product, though it still should have an ISBN number and copies sent to the Copyright

The Cover: If possible you should have a well illustrated cover which should ideally be laminated and which will catch your hoped-for reader's eye on the bookshelf.

The Layout: The most important aspect of any book is that it should look professionally produced. On pages 21-25 are examples of an attractive and open set up for the first few pages of your book.

Title Page: Remember that your book will have to shoulder its way to prominence on a bookself with many others, so apart from having an attractive and striking cover that begs someone to pick it up, it needs a title which of itself will make a browsing person pick it up out of sheer curiosity. You obviously appear as author, as you will also appear as Publisher.

Copyright Page: Apart from the copyright symbol and the copyright protection paragraph, this is where your ISBN number should appear. If you are only producing your book for private consumption of family and friends you do not really need one, but if the book is to be on sale through bookshops and in libraries, then it is important to have a ISBN, as most shops order from a Whitaker's microfiche, and without one you simply will not appear on that list.

This is also the page on which to put acknowledgements and any other snippets of information you wish to impart to your reader.

Contents Page: The details here are obvious, though it should be remembered that it is best that the name of each poem appears on the left of the page, number on the right.

Dedication: To look effective it is best to have the page immediately following the contents page blank except for virtually everyone is far too close to their own work to be able to evaluate the quality of it – you need an editor. Even if the person you choose is only someone whose opinion you value and respect, you should have someone decide with or for you, what you are to include in your book (by the time this process is complete you may well no longer have any respect for the person's opinion and have lost a friend, but you will have had your book edited!).

Your next task is to obtain an ISBN number from J Whitaker & Sons Ltd, 12 Dyott Street, London WC1A 1DF. You must send them your name and address (as publisher) together with a copy or 'pull' of your title and copyright pages, once they have proof that your name is to appear as publisher they will send you your number. Then you will need to get a bar code from Service Codes, 2 The Rise, Eastgate, Hornsea, Yorkshire HU18 1DR – they will need your ISBN number together with the price of the book and will want to know whether you need a positive, negative, or a bromide of your bar code – this last information will be given you by your Printer.

Do not rush into publication with the first Printer you approach – get quotations from as many different Printers as you can and ask to see copies of similar work they have previously produced – not every Printer knows how to print books, some are hard-pressed to produce a dozen satisfactory letterheads! Personally, after 25 years and 11 Printers, the best I have found is the one that printed this book (and all the NPF books), David Archard of Meon Valley Printers, whose full address appears on the last page.

Don't over-estimate the number of copies you are going to need. Unless you have a large private market for your book you will be hard-pressed to move more than, say, 200 copies.

Once you have chosen a Printer you need to consider:

company!

I am here specifically speaking of *poetry* books for I have no experience in other fields of publication, but where they are concerned I have never had the pleasant experience of meeting someone who has had a book published through one of these joint ventures and made one penny profit. Who has ever even seen his initial outlay covered. I have, however, received hundreds of letters over the years from people, disgruntled with wonderous financial promises, weighed against pecunary actuality. If there is out there *one* vanity press; *one* joint venture publishing house which can prove that it has ever published a poetry book for anyone and that client made a profit or even just covered his outlay, I shall be pleased to hear from them and shall praise the name of that company to the rafters, nay to the very heavens!

A final word on vanity or joint-venture publishing. The main aspect to remember is that no matter how much you are asked to pay as your 'contribution' to publishing costs you are also paying 100% of that publisher's profit margin which itself seldom falls below 'the ridiculously high and greedy'.

Often the eventual book is substandard in quality and is read by very few, (other than you and your own family) whatever promises are made in the blurb to get you to part with your money.

So really, rather than almost guaranteeing yourself a lot of expense and disappointment, you are better off

SELF-PUBLISHING: It is only comparatively recently (in the poetry world) that self-publishing has been looked upon as anything other than a sop to the poet's own ego, for all the fact that many well-known writers have had to resort to it to get their work off the ground. Where poetry is concerned, though, you need to bear in mind that

£2,000 (be generous with the £1,500 book) plus £2,347 and you get £4,347 . . . but she had paid out £8,000!

While I'm on the subject, a very similar ploy is used by certain companies who invite poems for an anthology – no, you don't have to pay *one penny* to have your work published if accepted. Your poem will appear in the anthology which you may purchase for £x.

Most people on being told that they've a poem in an anthology will buy a copy (or two). When you get yours you will find its production is a bit cheap-and-nasty, the poems are crammed together (to get as many possible on a page) and most of what you read will be poor quality.

Even the most gullible must have got there by now. Cram as many poems from as many different people as you can between the covers (say a hundred) and then charge £5 a copy for an anthology which costs you some £1.37 to produce, do that as often as you can each year – and go to the bank.

There is *of course* a place for vanity publishing. There are those who are not interested in others' opinions of their poetry, but simply want to leave a small booklet for their grandchildren (or someone similar). There are those who have no interest in any 'poetic standing', but simply *must* see their work in print whatever the cost. Both could no doubt do better through a private Printer, but if they don't want to involve themselves with their book, then the VP are for them.

No, the damage I feel the VP and some share-publishers do, is to tell people how wonderful their poetry is (in an attempt to get them to part with money) when in fact the poetry in question is often little better than very weak doggerel. The number of aspiring poets who have written to me over the years, proudly telling me how highly "so-and-so" praised their work, only to have that so-and-so turn out to be a real 'so-and-so' from a Vanity Press

CHAPTER III

So often I have people write to me saying that they are unemployed/short of money or in need of funds for some charity and therefore want to publish their first book of poetry in support. Invariably this innocent and laudable suggestion is followed by the statement that one or other of the

PUBLICATION-SHARING OR VANITY PRESS have quoted them a price they cannot possibly afford and, can I please advise them. My advice *always* has to be, "you might make a very small profit if you 'self-publish' but I have never met anyone doing so via the route you intend."

Let me say as loudly as I possibly can, no matter how much one of these companies may promise you a huge "share-in-the-profits," or an immense and "better-than-anyone-else-offers, royalties," there is most unlikely to be any of either. The companies are there first and foremost to make money for themselves, and I can assure you they are the only ones who *ever* do. Think about it for a moment . . . it is difficult enough to make a small profit if you self-publish and keep your costs to a minimum, so how can you *possibly* expect to make a profit on the back of paying someone else's salary and overheads and gas bill first?!

Some little while ago a lady wrote to me to say that (after I had previously warned her) she had just received a 'royalties' cheque and was "over-the-moon".

We then, together, did the sums . . . she had paid £8,000 to have her book published – she sent me a copy of the book in question which, on inspection, would have cost no more than fifteen hundred pounds to produce. She had now received a cheque for £2,347 royalties. Add together

Other than that? Well, I was asked by one of those same major bookshops of which you speak (when I canvassed them to buy books) to send them half a dozen different covers – not whole books, you will notice, just their covers. They were to choose their selection, not from a deep understanding of poetry and the poetry market place, but by whether the covers were pretty enough – a case of commercialism gone rogue if I ever heard of one!

At that point I felt like throwing in the proverbial sponge. Of helping whelk breeders in the gusty and forlorn outer somewhere, or perhaps of founding the first licenced parlour opened specifically for the vivisection of those faceless literary directors whose names (in our nightmare) always begin with the letters . . .

is to be found in the experience of Simon Armitage. Some of his poetry is to me of the most annoying and aggravating genre, for he is one of the few poets I know of today for whom I feel the greatest envy – that I have not written many of his poems myself.

OK, so Simon's a fine poet with a fresh original voice (I don't mean his accent) and the fact that he can obviously *hear* what he writes. But in being a good poet, does that make him poetically aware enough of the poetry of others to become editor at Chatto & Windus? He might be able to *write* poetry well, but can he judge it? Has he that completely 'objective' ear? The years of experience it takes to be consciously objective, rather than subconsciously subjective?

Fair enough, he may prove to be an outstanding editor, but, "the better the poet the worse the judge," has more than once been proved.

This smacks of commercial hype, as does the request by some Brewery for him to take part in a lager advert, because he sounds Northern and working class (to rhyme with 'lass'). But not to worry, I gather from the Saturday morning *Telegraph Magazine* (2nd Sept '93) one of the Brewery's Ad' men is to write a suitable poem!

It is only to be hoped that Simon, shekels not withstanding, continues to keep his integrity by turning down such insanity.

"But the major bookshops buy the poetry big publishers bring out," I hear you chorus. *Of course* they do! You don't honestly believe that many shop poetry-book-buyers are employed for their knowledge of poetry – *do* you!?

So how does it work? The Establishment makes a fuss over a poet. Those interested in poetry (the vast majority, non-poets) go into bookshops and out of curiosity order a copy of the book. The Establishment hype has worked. The bookshop fills the orders.

as her goal) one of our finest serious 'funny' poets. But not if that development is forced to take place in the Establishment fish-bowl, where you are expected to play its game – Poetry's Olympics, orchestrated by those who would have you run the marathon when your accomplishment is the 110 metres high hurdles.

Helped by editors? Becoming publically appreciated for a performance quirk, the poet risks being typecast by editors who will only accept work through which *they* recognise that poet, however much that poet may wish to branch out, diversify, develop – has this already happened to Wendy?

Let me give you another example which might make my musings easier to follow . . . Spike Milligan CBE was for so many years the king of scatterbrain comedy, but he has also written some extremely meaningful and well constructed serious poetry, yet when he has performed such work it is still always the case that some prune (normally many of them one-after-another) will come up to him and say, "I liked the Goons!" Or complain – strident sotto voce – that he wasn't being "funny enough." To watch him visibly shrivel as each new prune approached has been sadness itself and I could happily have shaken each one of them until their teeth fell out!

In this instance it's a question of someone who has been renowned as *The* archetypal funny man, experiencing difficulty when wishing to have his well written serious poetry accepted. Anyone else should, you would think, find it easier. But when that poetry has also yet to really develop, it is asking far too much of us all, although the Establishment can't see that.

Would that the fine poet Phoebe Hesketh had received half the acclaim from these self-appointed manufacturers of our standards.

Another example of gaffes by the art world hangers-on

pick up (should they exist) all the weaknesses so well hidden by our actor.

But radio? Blind poetry? Here again, the glib, amusing, throw-away-punch-line poem may well work, but you have to be even more careful not to use totally obscure, poet-chatting-to-own-navel, poetry because the listener has only this one single occasion on which to glean all the poem has to offer – no body language nor facial expressions to help, just blind words. Having said that, radio can offer the finest arena for poetry there is – just the words and you – nothing to come between, nothing *is* between, you and the words. No distraction from your own interpretation of what you hear.

Perhaps the best example of the 'funny poet' phenomenon is Pam Ayres (though she was gracious enough to write to me admitting she knew nothing about poetry, and has been heard to contradict someone referring to her as "a poet").

Stage and TV audiences *adore* her. She is funny, she is risqué, she is almost-nearly but never-quite, very rude. She has a 'roguish, come you hither m'love and we'll . . .'! On stage she is *tremendous* fun.

But it isn't what she *writes*, but how she puts it across, that counts. When she was published what she offered *didn't* work – Pam Ayres, the bundle of nudge-nudge- -fun-in-person, was simply not, on the page.

Some of Wendy Cope's work is hilariously funny – in recital. But she hasn't yet developed her full potential as a poet. She is at present a performer. Most of her work (not as yet being of sufficient substance to stand the microscopic eye of publication) relies on her visual, or at least verbal, presence. On a page, without her aura, her poetry's lack of maturity becomes too apparent.

Left alone to experiment in the privacy of her art and helped by editors, she no doubt will achieve the development and become (something which Pam Ayres never pretended of the major publishing houses (let us call it 'Unser & Stanton plc' so it shall not be confused with itself) announced it had a new Poetry Editor, a Mr C Nepytis. The following weekend in one of the supposedly highly respected daily nationals Mr CN gave a long interview in which he waxed profound about the difficulties of being accepted (chosen) for the U&S Poetry List; the fact that everybody who had previously been chosen (by other Poetry Editors) was now suspect . . . and that it was almost impossible to get accepted for publication by this illustrious publisher. The following weekend there appeared in a equally supposedly-highly-thought-of and respected Sunday newspaper the announcement of a 'new person' who had just miraculously been accepted by U&S for their "almost-impossibly-difficult-to-get-onto-list-of-poets." Most certainly he or she must be a poet of exceptional class. His name? Mr Nepytis – now where have I heard that name before?

I sometimes wonder why it is that the Establishment have so much difficulty differentiating between a poet and a personality. There used to be the book or the stage recital as a means of communicating what a poet had to offer. Now the choice is somewhat broader in that there is the book, stage and radio or television (fair enough, you can argue convincingly that stage=TV, but radio is very different). Three basic potential poetic outlets, then.

A poem that works well on stage where it has the assistance of the poet/reader's acting ability, personality and body language to put it across, may well be steeped in poetic faults which are submerged beneath the personality behind the performance, but as long as its effect is 'immediate' then there is a good chance it will work for an audience because of the persona of the performer. A poem for publication in a book doesn't need to have the attribute of immediacy – the reader can return to it time and time again to glean from it all the poet has to offer, but by doing so will gone on before he had become so expert . . . think of yourself as a juggler. A juggler with words! As a poet your work can only improve (appear effortless and lack contrivance) if you continually practice and experiment with your art.

You cannot each morning (or at least, very, very few are able to) awake with the idea that "before breakfast I shall write a well constructed poem." You might write a bit of weak doggerel, but poetry? *Every* morning?! A poet's life consists of a continual jotting down of odd ideas, odd phrases, while awaiting the muse. So be patient – that well written poem *will* untangle itself from the dross of the every-day.

One thing you will learn very early on in your career is the need for persistence – unfortunately it is very difficult to find even one editor as convinced of your poetic genius as you yourself, and so you need to be forever doing the rounds of submitting work to various editors and, however often you are faced with a rejection slip, doggedly continue to send out your work. Hopefully acceptance will eventually follow – unless of course your poetry is *so* dire there comes a time when the number of editors you have written off as "idiots with no poetic knowledge" (because they will not accept your masterpiece) exceeds the number of poetry magazines available to you, then it is time for you to take stock.

But how *do* those poets whose work is published by the 'big' publishers get taken up? Do all those, acclaimed by the Establishment, really deserve to be so?

The answer to the second part of that question is of course a resounding NO – they do not *always all* deserve the acclaim – and the answer to the first part, a loudly resounding and continuing state of puzzlement!

Let me simply muse aloud and you, draw conclusions as and how you may (good luck!) . . . not very long ago one come to the thorny problem of

__WHAT TO SUBMIT__: Your first consideration must be that *poetry is communication*. If you are writing for your family and friends it doesn't matter if your subject and the way you approach that subject says absolutely nothing to anyone who wasn't either there (at the scene of your poem), or to whom the subject isn't personally known. The poem you have written is specifically aimed at an audience which will enjoy it whether it has the slightest poetic merit or not. But if you are to submit work for possible *publication*, then it follows that the poem you submit must not only have the ability to interest your hoped-for reader out there, but also have poetic merit – be written well *as* poetry. For it is 'out there' that you will either become recognised as a poet of some worth, or dismissed as a mere scribbler of weak verse. So, it isn't *what you write* that is important, but, out of what you write, *what you decide to submit* and how you submit it.

Finally, what do you want from your verse? For this will decide

__WHERE TO SUBMIT YOUR POETRY__: The dream that you will overnight become a world famous poet, lauded from one end of your high street to the other, just won't come true. For even the best poet the road to acknowledgement is long, uphill, rocky and full of pitfalls, so you need to be ever-mindful of the three Ps – **P**ractice, **P**atience and **P**ersistence. The other week I was at Covent Garden in London where I saw a juggler; he was asking passers-by to lend him items with which to juggle.

As I watched him deftly catching those items and then effortlessly sending them in a parabola above his head, I thought of the hours of practice-and-failure, practice-and-failure, practice-and . . . success! that must have don't alter it. Never put more than one poem on a page (however short the poem) and always present it on an A4 sheet of white paper with your full name and address in the top right hand corner of the page.

Remember that 'double spacing' means double line spacing, <u>not</u> double spacing between words!

Never send the only copy of your poem, always make sure *you* have a copy, but equally don't send a carbon or photocopy, always a clean top copy.

Don't send one A4 sheet with your name on it, another with the poem's title, another with the poem, all with a stiff backing card, Recorded Delivery with the instruction, "Don't Bend." It is a fine way to antagonise an editor before he has even opened your missive.

Remember, you may be able to read your writing, but probably no-one else can. Not only should you always type your poems, but you should type your covering letter as well, for there is nothing more frustrating than receiving page after page of a totally indecipherable and illegible letter.

Don't submit your work with a scruffy second-hand s.a.e. for its return. No editor has time to discover that your envelope won't stick down and search for the Sellotape, then discover that the stamp you *should* have stuck on the envelope is somewhere in your package; and s.a.e means <u>stamped</u>, <u>addressed</u>, envelope, not an envelope sans name, sans address, sans stamp, sans, in fact, anything!

All in all make your editor's life as easy and simple as you would like yours to be, were you in his place.

It is often useful to see a magazine to which you intend submitting work, so write to the editor, not telling him to send you a back copy, but asking how much a copy costs and enclosing an s.a.e. so he can tell you – whenever you write to anyone enclose an s.a.e. for their answer.

So now you know how (and how not) to submit work we

CHAPTER II

I have never met the poet who (however dogmatically he may claim the opposite) does not wish other people to read, enjoy, and make complimentary noises about, his poetry. Many, having received such from their family and friends, find it difficult to accept a completely different reaction when their poetry is subjected to the blistering light of public day – the knowledgeable poetic public 'out there'.

The critical acclaim of family and friends (the captive audience) is normally nothing short of worthless when taken as a yardstick of our poetic genius . . . or otherwise!

There is of course nothing wrong with writing poems that are simply for your own enjoyment or that of your loved ones and friends, but such work should be kept in its proper place and not submitted for possible publication. What point is there in presenting a poem that says only what has been said a hundred times before in the self-same words; or where the rhymes are forced or weak and archaic; or the poem is so obscure it says nothing to anyone other than yourself or those very close to you? But I jump the gun so to speak, I should start with how to prepare your work for

PRESENTATION: Imagine, if you will, the hard-pressed editor faced with reams of letters, poems and queries, every morning. As he goes through the daily turmoil of his mail he comes across a thick wodge of hand written, pencil-corrected poems (40 or even 100 of them!) with a covering note which tells him to read them. Imagine, if you will, his response! If you want your poetry read then you must submit it as though you are proud of it! Each poem must be typed – if you make a mistake retype the poem, awaiting publication into the foreseeable future, or, he has enjoyed your book, but it doesn't fit into his editorial criteria – but that is only the beginning of it!

Some editors, out of some misguided sense of not wanting to hurt a poet's feelings, say that what has been submitted is "well crafted" or "very enjoyable" or that the "rhymes hold together well," or some similar and meaningless nonsense, only to top it off with telling the writer that he can't (for as many different reasons as a dog has fleas) publish it. You *must* remember it is the easiest thing in the world to say 'nice things' about someone's work when you have not to justify its publication! Too often someone writing in that vein means that he . . . hasn't enjoyed the work at all, finds it poorly crafted, the rhymes inverted, archaic and excruciating, and wouldn't publish it if it were the last poem in the world. But, with this empty praise reverberating through every pore of the poet's ego the work is resubmitted to some new, unsuspecting editor, together with a note telling *him* how well it has been received elsewhere! If the poet is fortunate he will get a reply telling him the truth – for what earthly benefit is there to any poet in telling him that he writes well, when in fact you know what you should be advising is the taking up of crochet, pig farming, wellie wanging – anything in fact, other than the continual battering to which he is subjecting the poor long-suffering Muse!

they are poor judges, only that they are unable to express what their emotional judgement has told them. (You try listening to your two favourite pieces of music and then explain - convincingly - why you prefer one to the other). There are most definitely times when an emotional approach to a poem can warp or unhinge coolly logical assessment. Take someone recently bereft of a small child or parent; faced with a poem on either subject their reaction may swing from extreme hostility to, or love for, the poem. No-one can be blamed for not recognising the emotional content of their reaction to a given poem. Though it is possible to train oneself to block out such an approach and judge solely from an "is it well written," standpoint, to say that one can completely disregard all emotional awareness is perhaps a moot point.

I'm sure you'll appreciate that when I talk of editors easily appreciating that a poem is of a high standard I am talking of work which manifestly is. When it comes to the run-of-the-mill poetry then problems occur. So much such work is border-line. Such a poem may say enough to one editor to justify its publication, while the same poem leaves another utterly unmoved. Again we are talking more from an emotional or experience level, than from one of quality. You must also appreciate that a few editors have not the slightest poetic knowledge, having set up a magazine with the sole intent of publishing their own work and that of their friends which the 'proper' magazines have found it impossible to digest! Fortunately these magazines seldom enjoy the longevity of more than one grape harvest - the poetry world being a richer place for their demise!

THE EDITORS' LIES: And so we come to the third question. There is many a genuine editor who will write to you saying that he "likes your work but can't publish it." He has either run out of funding, genuinely has a back-log

Where other art forms are concerned you will often hear the expression "he has a brilliant pair of hands," as though it were they, rather than the artist's mind and visual ability that create. In fact 'they' do no more than carry out the commands from the mind. You'd never hear that said of the poet!

The poetic art is more personal because it is the direct expression of the poet's own thought patterns. It is hardly surprising then that the individual poet is much more defensive of his art (his own mind) than one who can blame his tools for any 'blemish' not acceptable to his audience!

DIVERGING JUDGES AND EDITORS: To answer the second of the questions we must look at how we assimilate poetry. If someone were asked to judge the best laid out shopping list it would be a simple task – assessing the logical order, the neatness etc. But poetry is not judged solely through the audio/visual senses, it also involves the emotions and that is where the problems of 'difference of opinion' occur.

You can guarantee that most judges will recognise a well written poem that speaks to its audience with clarity and a sure poetic form. But ask each judge to write down *why* it is a fine poem and there will, without doubt, be areas where there is a divergence of opinion. Ask each to make a list of the order in which say ten, well-written, poems should be placed and you can be certain they will differ one from the other – why? In the final analysis it is the striking of an emotional chord and sub-conscious memory which give the judgement, often without the individual being aware of the process that is taking place. We are all aware of the situation where a group of judges, when asked why they have picked a particular poem, were unable to give a logical answer. This doesn't necessarily suggest that

CHAPTER I

Since 1967 I have been helping poets get into print, on to radio and tv, and advising them where their (sometimes very good, sometimes utterly dire) poetic efforts are concerned. During that time I have continually been asked three questions:

Why is poetry so much more a personal art form than any other?

Why does the opinion of editors and judges differ so widely?

Why do so many editors write and tell me my work is good but they are not prepared to (can't) publish it?

INDIVIDUALITY OF POETRY: From my own experience as an artist, wood carver and sculptor, I know it is far easier to accept comments (favourable or not) about one's painting or sculpture, than one's poetry. With all other art forms there is a question of distance. A painting is a *likeness of* something (at arms' length, as it were), but a poem is not a mapping out of a likeness of something but a putting down of *one's own feelings about* that something.

Then there are the materials – the paint, the brushes, the chisels, the hammer – with which the mind is expressing an image. In doing so the materials themselves help distance the artist from his work. The poet has a pen, pencil, typewriter or wp, through which to communicate his thoughts, so it can be argued that both the poet and the artist use materials to convey their message, but the artist is not using words – the direct expression of his mind.

Dedicated to those who have (at times) tried to make my life impossible, for through their efforts I so much more appreciate all who have helped to make it a wonderful and somewhat exciting experience.

Chapter VII
   A Matter Of Form (by Howard Sergeant MBE)   53
   Blank Verse   57
   Free Verse   57
   Sprung Rhythm   58
   Concrete Poetry   60

Chapter VIII
   Terminology For Measures   63
   Feet Most Often Used In English Verse   64
   Types Of Rhythm   66
   Metre   67
   Metrical Systems   67
   Metrical Licences   69
   Extrametrical Syllables   71
   Classification Of Rhymes By Place In Poem   75
   Classification Of Rhymes By Syllables   76
   Poetical Licence In The Use Of Rhyme   77
   Other Rhyme Forms   80

Chapter IX
   Ability   83
   The Poet Laureate   84

Chapter X
   Letters   86

Chapter XI
   Art Insanity   92
   The Poetry Society   93

Useful Addresses   102

* * * *

CONTENTS

Chapter I
   Individuality Of Poetry   1
   Diverging Judges And Editors   2
   The Editors' Lies   3

Chapter II
   Presentation   5
   What To Submit   7
   Where To Submit Your Poetry   7

Chapter III
   Publication-Sharing Or Vanity Press   14
   Self-Publishing   16
   Poetry Magazines   26
   Small Publishing Houses   28

Chapter IV
   The National Poetry Foundation   29
   The Rosemary Arthur Award   35
   Recitals   36
   Grants   37

Chapter V
   Local Branches   45
   Setting Up A Poetry Group   47
   Poetry Competitions   48

Chapter VI
   What Is Poetry?   50

(cont:)